C000090301

# Retrace

# Retrace

## STELL'S JOURNEY

ASH V

PARTRIDGE

Copyright © 2020 by Ash V.

Library of Congress Control Number:      2020904208
ISBN:        Hardcover      978-1-5437-5397-4
        Softcover      978-1-5437-5395-0
        eBook      978-1-5437-5396-7

All rights reserved. No part of this book may be used or reproduced by any means, graphic, electronic, or mechanical, including photocopying, recording, taping or by any information storage retrieval system without the written permission of the author except in the case of brief quotations embodied in critical articles and reviews.

Because of the dynamic nature of the Internet, any web addresses or links contained in this book may have changed since publication and may no longer be valid. The views expressed in this work are solely those of the author and do not necessarily reflect the views of the publisher, and the publisher hereby disclaims any responsibility for them.

Print information available on the last page.

**To order additional copies of this book, contact**
Toll Free +65 3165 7531 (Singapore)
Toll Free +60 3 3099 4412 (Malaysia)
orders.singapore@partridgepublishing.com

www.partridgepublishing.com/singapore

# CONTENTS

# CHAPTER ONE

## *It started out rough -Childhood*

*Childhood is supposed to be the most memorable
thing for every individual. Childhood is what
makes or breaks a person and who they turn
out to be. Loss at childhood totally defines a
complete change of heart and mentality.*

Stella Marie's world had come to a complete stop. It felt like she was in a *Nightmare on Elm street* instalment an old horror/ thriller movie from the eighties. Campbell street felt that way on the day her mom died that was the day her nightmare felt real. CANCER! More definitively. Was the FREDDY KRUEGER, which came and ate her mother alive in just a few short months? Sitting under her mother's elevated coffin and playing with her dolls the little girl had no understanding that her mama is gone forever. Painful and dreadful is the feeling of loss. Mama, why did you leave me? Her constant question that was left lingering on her mind was painful and it tore a child from the comfort from a mother's touch. Clinging to her daily was all she could remember. Like a baby Joey in a mother kangaroo's pouch; Stella Marie was comfortable in the presence of her mother yet now cancer had taken her away. She could not feel anything because her innocence held her from even the thought that her mother would not wake up again.

Everyone was dressed in black but she chose Emerald green because that was Mama's favourite colour. Mama loved Emerald green dresses it reminded her of her mother. People were crying and throwing flowers into the coffin but she was sitting and talking to her dolls like it was just another day. Daddy was busy

1

attending to everyone at Mama's wake. It didn't occur to her that she was supposed to be dressed in black or that she was supposed to cry. She just couldn't do it. *Mama can't be gone because she's asleep and she would wake up later and play. She always takes afternoon naps and it was afternoon. Right?* Her own personal thoughts filtered the sadness and instilled her with hope. Hope that Mama was about to wake up. Hours later though Mama was driven in a black and long hearse while she was still laid down in that box.

Moments later the car pulls up at cemetery where everyone gathered around as they sealed the box and lowered her down into a deep and dark hole. It kicks in right there for the little eight-year-old Stella Marie, who breaks into pieces. "NO!! Mama come back, get mama out of there! Daddy, she belongs with us, she belongs with me! DADDY! Why are they taking her away from us? STOP!!!" She screams and falls to the ground almost rolling in six feet under together with Mama. Daddy pulled her back before she could fall in. They dug up the sand over the box that mama was in. Took her some time but she figured out what the box was called. *A coffin.*

They sang hymns that suggested mama went to the big man in the sky. Hymns that had words such as *Nearer my God to thee, nearer to thee, Angel to beckon me, nearer to thee.* The more they sang it the more she cried and screamed her lungs out. The deeper it felt that mama's body had gone away. No more could she hold her hands and no more could she hear her voice. Mama is gone now she said goodbye and the devastation kicked in as the hymn was repeatedly sung. DEATH had come and told her that it had taken away apart of her. The part that connected her to this world. That held her for nine months in her womb. Spent fourteen hours in labour and also in extreme excruciating pain to get out of her so she could see her breathe her first breath and have her first cry.

While Stella Marie had to see mama take her last breath and cry her last tear as she said goodbye to her twenty-four hours before they lowered mama, six feet under and raised Stella Marie's brokenness to the next level. She struggled to come to terms with loss but mama struggled with a lot more. Mama struggled for ten months in pain and bleeding out loads of blood but all she could care about was her little sweet pea. How she was not going to be there when she is all dressed up to go to prom or when she graduated. How it would have been like to send her off to college and hug her while she cried to say goodbye. How it would have been to be there when she had her first love or her first heartbreak. Even more, the day she walked down the aisle in a beautiful dress as Daddy walks by her side to give her away to a man who would love her just as much as both of them did.

She did not even get to see her take her first Holy Communion. Time was cut short for mama but that only meant a new journey for both daddy and Stella Marie.

Daddy was still there with her picking up all the pieces that mama's demise had left them both in. Nathan aka daddy had to admit he felt lost. How was he going to raise this little eight-year-old all by himself, when all he did was work and bring home the money? He never knew the insights on what it was like to do the everyday job of a mother. He was really young when he was left to fend for himself when he was only fifteen. He started working to support his family because his dad had died and he was the oldest among three siblings. He did odd jobs due to his lack of education after he dropped out of school. Now a man who spent a lot of his life working had to start understanding the idea of raising a child. Not having much of a childhood himself and having his wife handle her all the while, it felt surreal for him to even understand the concept of not just financially supporting or hugging her and saying I love you but covering the love lost. The void that her Mama's death had left behind. Not only did he have to father her but he also had to have a mother's heart.

A challenge that most men would have run away from. This was a challenge Nathan took up because he loved his daughter just as much or even more than he loved his wife. They are diamonds in his eyes. Now he had a little diamond to polish and keep close to his heart as long as he lived. This was the promise he made to his dying wife and to himself. The splitting image of her mother was what she turned out to be every little bit, from her smile to her angry face. How was he going to be strong and take care of her when she constantly reminded him of his dead wife? As her father he had to be selfless. The day had come for him to learn more about being selfless, it was the first day after the funeral that anything close to her presence was completely wiped away. He had to start somewhere, so he started by cooking her a meal.

She sat in the kitchen hardly touching her food. In fact, Stella Marie did not eat even a bit of what daddy had cooked. Nathan felt very discouraged and tried his best to talk to her. She always had so much to say but today was an exception. Today it was a really emotionally cloudy day for his little angel. All he saw her do was stare at an empty chair opposite of her.

The chair mama used to sit on. "Baby piglet, are you not hungry? I thought you loved bacon and eggs or did you want some Chinese food I could grab some for you. "He offered. Stella said nothing in response. She just stared blankly at the chair. Then she suddenly fell to the ground and started crying. He quickly rushed over to her and knelt down as he held her in his arms. She was breaking apart and he felt it just as much. He was breaking down too as he felt her pain. They both lost their angel.

Mama was the light that brightened their home and now it felt so gloomy. It's like the devastation kicked in even more as she cried out, screaming in tears. He couldn't take it to see that his little baby was broken. She was in anguish and he had no idea how to make it all go away. There was no way to make any of this go away. He was in just as much pain but he had to put her pain first. That's what a parent does they put their child's needs before their own. It was her loss that mattered more than his. She was just a child she just learned a few years ago how to write, read and feel.

Now she had to pour all these feelings out because she had no idea how to control those feelings. She was too sheltered by her mama. Dearest daddy had no idea how to nurse the emotional wounds of an eight-year-old girl. He did not know how to even let her know, how he felt about losing the love of his life. They met twice and the second time they met sealed the deal for both of them.

Nathan William L. That was the name in his ID. Never knew what the L stood for he just assumed it stood for love. He met Rosemary Matthews at a party when they were sixteen, he told her the same thing to start a conversation. They dated up until she was eighteen and heartbreakingly, she had to go away for college so she had to break up with him because she was afraid of long-distance relationships. He never saw or heard from her again till she was thirty-two with a son from a previous marriage that had ended badly. Eventually her husband had died. Then has fate had, had it Nathan and Rosemary met at a party again years later and the rest is history. They were soulmates and fate had proven it. Her son had not looked her up again as he lived with his grandmother from his father's side. So, Nathan and Rosemary had little Stella Marie their pride and joy. She was the one and only for them because she was more than enough for them.

As he got reminded of the day she was born, he carried her off the ground, laid her down on the sofa and sat beside her.

"Goodbyes are not forever, we will be reunited again in heaven one day but until then, mama has left her love for us both. Love always remains. "He reassured her. She laid her down on his lap as she teared gently. Those words meant a lot to her. It lifted her spirits to know that mama maybe physically gone but her spirit lives on in both of them. Her love remains in both of them. It felt for a moment that he had gotten through to her and it felt so good. She was comforted and that's all he needed to help him to keep going. To be her daddy when she needed him the most. To put her needs before his. That's what daddies do. They love. He never fully felt the love of a father but he did receive the love of a mother. All he had to do was be a father with a mother's heart. Boy that was hard! Hard work. "Rosemary, teach me how to love her like you did." He whispered under his breath and his watched daddy's baby piglet doze off. She looked so precious and calm. Like all her fears and sadness had come to a halt. This was only while she was asleep, how would he continue to keep her this way while she was awake. He felt tired and he needed some rest too so he slept off on the sofa as well.

She opened her eyes and she was in a train, mama was there with her, they were talking and laughing like they always did and then mama gave her a drink which happened to be her favourite, hot chocolate with marshmallows. They were on a train going somewhere but they did not know where. It just felt nice and it was not a matter where they were going. The train comes to a stop and mama gets off but tells her to stay in the train as she waves goodbye. The train keeps moving and she screams out "MAMA!" As she cries. She opens her eyes and she's in tears as she looks up at her daddy's shocked face. "Are you okay baby piglet?" He asks her. "Mama said goodbye daddy, she's left, she sent me on my way and she said goodbye." He lifts her up and hugs her as they both are seated on the sofa. It was her way of asking for release he thought to himself. A way to tell her daughter she's going to be fine. There is nothing to worry about. At least not at this point of her life. Loving her through it all was all that mattered to him.

LOVE! A father's love just as much as a mother's love had to be unconditional but human love always has conditions so how does one love unconditionally? Easy right just doesn't pick any faults on the other, just let them do whatever they want to. But what if whatever they want to is never safe for them. What if the people they choose to be in their lives is not good for them either? That's a painful load of things to worry about Mr Nathan. A whole load of things. How would he do this parenting all by himself? His mother did it right on her own but he felt scared. How can a father fill a void when a mother's the one who bonds and carries a child for nine months?

Especially, when all he did was work so hard and forgetting that providing money was not the only thing a child needed from her father, love is a requirement too. Showering love more importantly. The next day, it was another one to be thankful for. As long as one wakes up in the morning there is definitely something more for them to do. He reminded himself and his little piglet. Making breakfast and tidying up the house before Stella had woken up. He had no idea what it is his wife worked at every morning before his daughter woke up but then again, he did not have to even think about it back when she was around. The eight-year-old woke up at last.

"My little piglet are you ready for some bacon and eggs?" He asked with a huge grin. She did not even respond and just sat at the table. He figured that she was ready so he served her the dish. "Daddy I have not brushed my teeth. Mama would never serve me breakfast until she forced me into the bathroom to brush my teeth." His little girl informed him. "Well, okay then get to the bathroom little piglet or I am going to make bacon out of you." He said to her and forced her to the bathroom in a fierce voice but his facial expression was far from fierce. Nathan burst out laughing at his daughter causing her to laugh as well. He sang to her the brush your teeth song that he had made up. It was horrible, the fact that he had no proper lyrics except 'Brush your teeth little piglet' and absolutely no singing talent made it hilarious. Rosemary was a better singer than him for sure. She was laughing so hard, she almost choked on her toothpaste and that was all he needed to do. Make her laugh.

He admired his little piglet every moment he was with her. The way her laughter was so adorable and contagious. The way her eyes sparkled when he made her laugh and the way she held his hand when she was afraid of the sound of thunder. These moments and many others grew on him day by day as he spent more time with her. Nathan really started to feel his love grow for his daughter every single day. It was beautiful the bond they were building it's like the day he remembered first holding her in his arms in the hospital. The day she popped out of Mama. March 22nd. It was a precious moment. They celebrated her birthday every year since she was born and now Mama left even before they reached March, February the 8th. A month away was their little piglet's birthday. Nathan had no idea if celebrating was a good idea but he wanted to try. There was still a lot of time for her to heal till then. Baking a cake was his strong suit but planning a party, no way man, that was Rosemary's strong suit. She was the best party planner ever! So that would mean celebrating would not be the best idea either because it will only make her miss mama more. So there was not going to be a celebration maybe just aa continued bonding session. A more special one.

Handling her and getting back to work and had been really hard on Nathan but he was tactful and handled it pretty well. There were constant dreams of his late wife, where she reminded him to do things he might have forgotten and it felt so real like it's as if she still there helping him be his 'day planner' as he used to call her. A very important part of his life was his beautiful wife. She was the backbone for the family and now he had to pick up these broken pieces of bones and piece it back together and put both his heart and his little piglet's back together. Boy! That was going to be a challenge.

Weeks had passed and things seemed to get better for Nathan and Stella. He juggled work and being a daddy. Had to leave her with relatives at times but she adapted well so he had no worries. A very easy child she was. Did not give him much trouble at all. The only hard part of it all was getting her to go back to school. He tried convincing her countless times but she refused. Time for them both to get on with their lives. He taught her by showing an example, by bringing her to work one day and showed her that he was his usual self and she could be too. There's nothing that should hold one back from living their lives. Their lives mattered. They had to get on with it, so long as they keep moving, they're making mama proud he reminded her constantly.

On the first day he had to send her back to school, it was the toughest thing he had to do. She clinked to him like a koala bear. Getting her to enter her school ground was like sending her to the battle ground. His little piglet had no intention of ever inside. "Hon, you have to go back to school and let daddy go." He pleaded with Stella. She refused silently and held on tighter to her daddy. Her teacher Ms Gomez saw that she was holding on tightly and approached the duo to try and help.

With her soft and connecting approach she called out to her. "Stella, we have missed you sweetie, your friends have been waiting for you, for days. Come on, follow me sweetie. "She called her and amazingly she managed to get Stella to let go of her father and follow her. He was free to go to work now though he did not have the heart to leave her. She turned back to look at him three times until she reached the area towards her classroom. He left trusting she was in good hands.

# CHAPTER TWO

## *School- Class is in session*

*The first place that a child has to part from a
parent to go to is a school and when they are
too attached from a moment of complete and
utter pain to their parent, it's hard to let go.
It's hard for new journeys to begin when old
ones are still part of one's healing process.*

Stella Marie reluctantly entered her classroom at Saint
Anthony's. Ms Gomez gathered everyone to give her a warm
welcome back. Each of them were holding up signs to welcome
their friend back. Welcome back STELLA MARIE. One of the
signs read. Her best friend Rocket was the first to move forward
and hug her. ROCKET. Jeffrey Luke Carter, preferred to be called
by his nickname always, had met Stella Marie in kindergarten and
they clicked right away. He was the only one who reached out and
made friends with her when she refused to talk to anyone back in
kindergarten. He always had it rough back home. His mother, left
his dad and only took his sister with her just two years earlier. He
was just hardly getting used to first grade when it happened. His
father would always get drunk and get into fights and teach his son
that fighting was the only way out. Being tough always was better
than being smart he taught him. Rocket became the biggest bully
in school especially at his grade level and expected everyone to be
afraid of him and respect him.

The only one who he would never bully and never let anyone bully
is Stella Marie. He was her confidant and protector. Seeing her in
pain made him feel upset and he hardly knew how to feel. Stella
hardly even said one word or smiled at anyone. All she wanted

to do is sit in a corner and Rocket wanted to be right next to her. Nobody could understand their friendship. Why would a quiet and sweet girl like Stella be friends with a rowdy like Rocket? Their friendship was like no other it was more real than it looked. There was this sweetness to it that only two of them could understand. "Stella Marie, I'm always going to be here for you, I hope you know that." He reassured her and she just nodded her head in response. Math class had started and she was far from there. Her mind was switched off. She had no idea what the math teacher was even teaching. After class ended it was recess and she ran to the girl's toilet to spend her time there. Rocket tried to catch up to her but she was too fast for him so he just waited outside for her. Eventually she came out and he approached her. "I got you something to eat before our next class." He offered her a sandwich. "Rocket, thank you but I am really not hungry. I appreciate it but I just need time-" She wanted to complete her sentence but was interrupted by him. "Time, you had enough of, what you need is to do something fun so that you can move on with your life, don't you think that would be what your mother would want, Stella Marie!" He frustratedly mentioned. She cried and moved forward and rested her head on his chest as he wrapped his arms around her before bringing her to the school pond area where they would always hang out.

The pond is where kids would throw in coins to make a wish through the fish. That's what they believed, that the fishes would somehow grant their wish. By the pond was a playground and tables and benches where the kids could go to sit and have their lunches or study when the weather was good. Wherever Rocket went the kids would move away from there as soon as they saw him. He OWNED the ground he walked on. Totally owned it. "Talk to me Stella Marie, remind me why we became friends in the first place."

Rocket found a topic to spark a conversation. "Why don't you remember Rocket? You beat up Samuel Mack because he took my colour pencils and I was crying, you felt sorry for me because I was crying and you were intrigued by my silence. "She mentioned to him. He was intrigued by her use of the word intrigued. "I will never let anyone bully you I am a bully who won't bully his best friend so why would I let anyone. Who knew I would become the best friend of an awkward, weird and silent girl? "She laughed at that comment. That she was always a quiet and awkward girl till the she met Rocket he taught her confidence and made her feel it. She walked with her head held high gradually after they formed a friendship. They were each other's rock. They leaned on each other whenever either one was down. This is what best friends do right count on each other. No one would ever even think of coming near her because he was always there for her no matter what.

As the years had passed, Rocket became more and more obsessed with control. He wanted to control any kid he set his mind to do so and if they did not obey his ways, he would just make their life a living hell. Him and his group of friends who had no guts to ever go against him did everything he said. Taking kids lunches, putting their heads down toilet bowls, beating them up the normal bully stuff. It got really extreme but he would cover up his tracks really well as to not get caught. Unfortunately for him, the next nerd he picked on was not just any nerd. The smartest kid in school, Roderick Lee. Top scorer every single year. Roderick, lived with his step-dad and mother. His own father was not one who is even close to reliable at all. He actually abused his mother and him. Constantly beat up her up, hitting her head against a tree, tearing up her clothes. The woman bled half the time she had lived with him. Roderick was so little that all he could ever do was cry as he watched his mother get tortured by his father. One day his mother, Agnes, built up the courage to go to the cops and that day was the day their life changed completely when she met a wonderful cop by the name of Stan Ray. He literally saved the both of them from this torture and constant abuse. After their abuser was put behind bars and Roderick's mother managed to get a divorce from his father, she and Stan Ray started spending more time together and eventually fell in love. Six months later they got married and moved to his home, selling off the home she shared with her ex-husband. Roderick finally started getting the home life he deserved. Stan Ray taught him everything and gave him the father's love he never received from his natural father.

Going to school though was a whole other form of abuse. Roderick constantly got beaten up by Rocket and his bunch of goons. It was too exhausting but he never told his parents. He just let it go on and on. For only one reason, Stella Marie. Stan Ray and Nathan, her father were the best of friends. Stan Ray was always there for Nathan through it all since they were younger. He was Nathan's source of strength during Rosemary's funeral. Both him and her always ended up being playmates on the weekends when they hung out at his home. She would play normally with him and he had to admit he had the best of times when he was around her. They always had fun and laughter playing together and that made both their fathers' so happy. Agnes would cook up a storm of a meal for all of them and they would enjoy it together. The sad part was that when they went to school, she would not even stand up for him when Rocket did anything to him. She would just sit there and keep quiet. He cared about her so much but she was too blinded to care. Even when he saw her sit by herself and cry, he would approach her in concern and she would just ignore him right before getting up to walk away. Roderick eventually convinced himself that she was probably only nice to him to please her father.

For her sake though, he kept his constant bullying a secret from his parents. It was a hell of a secret to keep especially since he always had bruises on him and torn clothes. His wallet was constantly missing as well. He would just give some excuse and cover it up, like that he fell down on his way back and dropped his wallet on the way. No one lies to a cop and gets away with it though except Roderick Lee, well because Stan Ray believed that he was quite a clumsy little kid. It had hurt him. Not the part where Stan Ray saw him as a clumsy kid but the part where he had to constantly lie to his parents and get beaten up by miniature goons for the sake of an ungrateful little girl. He just believed that she was just in too much pain and had no time or tolerance to think of others feelings and he cut her some slack for that. Going through so much as a young child made him more sensitive towards others feelings and aware of others' brokenness, enough to understand their feelings and sacrifice his own. Bittersweet. One day Stan Ray noticed that his arms were bruised terribly and he was just sitting and watching his favourite show. "Son, could we talk?" He caught his attention. "Yes dad?" Roderick replied. "I think, bruises like that need to be treated and are not to be left like that. I'm going to get that treated for you and I want the truth."

Stan Ray suspected that his son was not being completely honest though he brushed it off more than a couple of times. Roderick finally confessed but he made Stan Ray promise that he would not tell Agnes anything about this. So, he did. He promised that he would never tell unless she found out on her own. He took care of his bruises using the first aid kit he had and mentioned that he might have to consult a doctor to make sure everything was completely fine. The next day when he visited the doctor, he got some medication and got treated for the bruises on his arm but the doctor also noticed the bruises on his body. "Roderick, do you recall where you might have received these bruises from?" Dr Javan was quite concerned if there was more to what he and his father mentioned earlier about the bruises being obtained from a fall. Stan Ray was shocked to see those extra bruises because Roderick did not mention that or show it to him. "Is there something you need to talk about or maybe you'd like to meet with Dr Ricardo, he's more..." Dr Javan was cut off by Stan Ray. "It's okay if we need to talk to Dr Ricardo, we will contact him directly, could we just get some medication and an excuse chit for today?" Stan Ray added.

"Very well then." Dr Javan responded. The drive home after the visit to the clinic was really quiet. Just music by Pink Floyd playing on the radio. Stan Ray's favourite band. "We have to do something about this Roderick." Stan Ray sparked a conversation. "NO! Please I am already a loser in school, being a tattle tale is even worst." Stan Ray stopped the car and turned to Roderick. "Do we have to wait till you are in grave danger until we decide to make this a report. Have no teachers observed this?" Stan Ray asks. Roderick nodded in agreement as he knows Ms Gomez has but he would always cover up for it. Stan Ray was upset that even though they had known, no one did anything to stop it but then again it was the victim who constantly covered it up.

Stan Ray accompanied Roderick to school after dropping Agnes off at work as he had made a promise to Roderick not to tell her anything as she would be really hurt. All she knew was that he fell down. Stan Ray wanted to have a chat with Ms Gomez, the teacher that always looked out for the kid's welfare. Made sure they were always in a good place in their educational walk. "Good morning Sir, I am Ms Gomez, you wanted to speak with me?" She approached them as they waited for her in the office where she usually was. "Have you seen the bruises on my son's hands?" He vigorously spoke up. "Dad, please." Roderick tried to calm him down. "No, none of you took any steps to look into the bullying that is going on here and the kids suffering in silence because they are scared. What is this?" Ms Gomez had close to nothing in response to that. "Sir, I assure you if Roderick were to tell us the complete story, we will deal with it right away." She finally spoke up. Stan Ray kept silent for a second before responding.

"If you don't get the goons who did this to my kid corrected, they will never change and will do worst as they grow older. If you don't do anything, I will." He said before he got up and led Roderick and himself out of her office. Stan Ray scanned the whole school looking for Rocket and saw Stella Marie with him. They were talking and laughing out loud. Stan Ray approached them even though Roderick was trying to stop him. "Come here, you." He pulled Rocket aside. Rocket looked scared as Stan Ray pushed him up against a wall to talk to him. Stella Marie was shocked and did not know how to react. "Do you want to end up behind bars for the rest of your life, kid?" He asked him and the scared little boy shook his head in disagreement." If I ever see any fresher bruises on my son, I will make sure you never leave a boy's home till you're eighteen.

"He threatened him. Ms Gomez was alerted and ran out to approach them. "I'm sorry Sir, if you ever do that again I would have to take action towards you, please leave." She said to him. Stan Ray stared at a fearful Rocket before leaving. Stella Marie quickly rushed to his side. "In my office, NOW!" Ms Gomez called out to him.

Rocket was warned by Ms Gomez and Principal Reed to never ever go near a mile of Roderick or else he will be suspended from school together with all his accomplices. Right after that incident, the atmosphere at school felt different every time Roderick walked past Rocket and Stella Marie. Stan Ray would meet Nathan on his own but he would never invite Stella Marie over to play with Roderick. He felt that it would be better if Roderick stayed away from her though his son did not feel the same way.

# CHAPTER THREE

———◦∕∕∕◦———

## *Time changes, Spots don't*

*People grow older but whether their attitude
changes really depends on them because not everyone
believes they are in the wrong even when they are.*

*T*hree years had passed and Rocket tried his best to taunt
Roderick but he had no guts because Stan Ray would always
show his face in school to indirectly warn Rocket that he was not
kidding when he said what he did. Rocket hated Roderick even
more. It was not just about bullying "anymore it was now a rivalry
which was of course one sided. Roderick had absolutely nothing
against him. The only thing was the girl he had considered a
best friend was Rocket's instead. She stopped talking to him
completely, after the whole incident with Stan Ray happened. It
saddened him, as to how she could just ignore him all these years.
They were eleven now and she had grown up pretty well, beautiful
in fact and he was still his nerdy old self. Rocket found many ways
to taunt him. He worked hard to ignore him constantly and just
focus on his studies. Rocket was literally only good at one thing in
school and that was to come up with evil plans to make Roderick's
life in school miserable. He just had this extreme jealousy towards
Roderick for some reason, like he felt so threatened by him. God
knows why. Bullying him could not work anymore so he found
another way. He somehow knew that Roderick had this utter
appreciation for Stella Marie, so he used that to his advantage.
The school dance was coming up and it was the best opportunity
to do something evil, that was all in his mind. EVIL! He had not
even changed a bit.

"Remember the plan, okay? All you have to do is tell him you want to go with the dance with him. I will handle the rest, with the guys." Rocket ran through his 'Evil' plan with Stella Marie, briefly. Stella Marie was reluctant but she could never bring herself to say no to her best friend, even if it meant hurting someone else. Stella Marie did as he said and approached Roderick during recess. He was sitting all alone, having a sandwich while reading a book like he always does. "Hey Roderick." She said as she sat down opposite of him. He looked up in shock as she had not spoken to or acknowledged him in three years. "Hey..." He responded. "What's up." He added. "Well... you know how the school dance is coming up and I was wondering if you would go with me?" He had nothing to respond to her because he was in state of shock. He thought to himself that she had not spoken to him in years and the first thing she asks him is to go to a dance with her? That is surprising! He does not dance though. It's not his thing. "Yes!" He responded quickly. What?! Why did he just agree so quickly? She was happy and gave him a quick hug before leaving. Rocket was watching from afar. He had a smug smile planted on his face. His evil plan was on its way to succeed. He was proud of his evil ways. What he was up to everyone would only get to know on the day of the dance.

Stella Marie was not looking forward to the dance as she was not proud of doing what she is about to. She was going to help humiliate an innocent boy who has been nothing but genuine and nice to her since they were younger. Yet it was Rocket who was ever really there for her so though she knew it was wrong to do what he was asking of her. The whole night after asking Roderick to the dance she could not sleep, she got up a couple of times to get a glass of water from the kitchen. Daddy heard her walking up and down so he was awoken.

"Baby Piglet, why are you up? Had a nightmare?" He asked. "Could not even sleep daddy." She replied. He just went over sat with her and leaned in to let her rest her head on his shoulder. "Something bothering you?" She nodded in agreement to his question. "I did something or maybe I am going to do something I feel is not so good for a friend of mine but it is something my best friend wants me to do and I can't say no because he is my best friend." Her daddy paused a while before responding. "Well sweetie if you feel it is not right, then you should tell your best friend that you do not want to do it. Nothing is worth going against your personal ethic. Live your life right and make the right choices okay? We only have one." He advised her. After that she decided to do the right thing within a second of her daddy's advice. She was going to tell Rocket that she would not carry out the plan and tell Roderick that she was not going with him without giving away Rocket's plans. That way it's a win, right? She would prevent Roderick from getting humiliated and Rocket from getting suspended for his hooligan plan.

*NO!* It was not that easy. Rocket refused to let her back out of the plan as he had already done everything to carry it out. She was stuck in a mix now.

She could not escape it anymore after agreeing to it in the first place. Why girl? Why can't you ever say no to this boy. There she went she backed out of backing out. He sweetly manipulated her into going ahead with it. "Look, you are not going to do anything, just bring him to the dance. There is nothing unethical in that." He assured her and immediately, she agreed. Immediately, that is how quick she always responds or agrees with him. He knew how to pull on her heartstrings how to make her feel like she had to obligated to everything he had to say and he was only a kid. The word cunning should be used for someone like him more than smart. When it comes to his studies, he always had help to make him look smart but when it came to his mischief, he did great on his own.

As the days got closer Stella Marie felt more and more uncomfortable but Rocket became more and more inspired. Emotions are always different when intentions are varied for each individual. Some are happy with evil intentions while others with a proper conscience will not be excited in witnessing another's humiliation. It's a struggle to please someone when one does not truly support an action. Stella Marie, struggled with this choice. She feared the worst for herself and the rest, regret is going to live within, oh she knew it for sure. When the day finally came, she could hardly eat or do anything. Daddy was starting to worry about her. She was pretty much dazing and staring at her food. "Earth to Stella Marie!!" Daddy caught her attention leading her to drop her fork on the table. "Are you alright, baby?" He asked her. She nodded and asked to be excused from the table and ran to her room. Daddy was confused and decided to give her some time to herself before probing her for answers. She sat up in her bed and she was crying because she was not sure why, was it because she was afraid or she felt pity for Roderick either way she wanted a way out of this whole plan. As she was breaking into pieces inside her room, daddy knocked her door. She pulled herself together and then opened up the door for him.

"Baby, if there is anything bothering you, I'm here to listen." He offered and all she could do was hug her daddy and cry. "I did something wrong daddy; I am going to do something wrong." She cried as she told him. He asked her to explain to him what that meant and she gave him the whole story. Daddy was shocked, he was not even aware of what had been going on and Stella Marie's involvement. Stan Ray had not told him anything. He decided to go straight to Stan Ray's house to talk about it. He brought Stella along because the dance was going to be happening that night and they had to stop the whole plan Rocket had stirred up. Unfortunately, when they reached the destination nobody was home at all.

They had probably gone out and then would drop Roderick off for the dance after. It was not too late because they would still meet him at the dance later, at least before Rocket does anything at all. Roderick was at the mall with his father and mother picking out a nice suit. He wanted to look like a grown up, yes, he had grown taller but he needed a new style. This nerd look would not work out at dance. It made him all the more insignificant which he had been absolutely used to. The poor boy struggled with his self-image based on how he had been treated all those years. Stan Ray chose a stunning blue suit for his son. He told him how dashing he looked in it and that it made him proud to see him looking so dashing. Pride of any form in a child's achievement or life's milestone, is an important part of their development. Especially when they are young instilling confidence is important, not overconfidence but just plain confidence and self-love. Stan Ray did that for Roderick he made him to be comfortable in his own skin over the years and he was not going to stop teaching him about self-love.

Boys and girls alike go through image issues and it all starts young. So, there he was, ready in his stunning suit for a date with a sweet girl who he had always admired. She had finally asked him to the dance and he was excited. Both his mother and father watched their little man looking so matured. He chose the suit and they were ready to make their way over to the dance as time had caught up.

Rocket was too, for a whole other reason. Creating madness and mayhem to make sure all his enemies face the worst even if they have not done anything to him. Dressing up in a raggedy old outfit handed down from his father. He was as sick as his old man. Always seeking out trouble and to make the worst of someone else's happiness. His old man did that to his mother and that is why she packed and left with his sister. She did not want her little girl to grow up in such an environment. She wanted to take Rocket too but he would not let her and he lied to him about it. Making it look like his mother never wanted him. The boy grew bitter towards her and almost everyone else. Hence, he found comfort in his bitterness. Building this great wall of China and a war zone within his own conscience. It could be stopped but his pride A.K.A the Great wall of China was just way too much to breakdown. It was time! Time to cause some havoc.

The kids finally arrived at school for the dance. One by one or rather two by two they entered in, all dressed up and excited for the event they had waited for. Stella Marie, did not want to go in she remained in the car with daddy afraid to even open up the door. "Honey, we will handle this okay? Once I see Stan Ray, I will approach him and warn Rod about this crazy plan that Rocket has." Her father reassured her. As she turned to look out of the window, she noticed that Rocket had already arrived with his goons. They were sneaking in by the back entrance of the school hall. Nathan noticed that Stan Ray's car was there and wanted to go into the school to look for him but was stopped by Stella. "Daddy let me handle this, it's my mistake to fix." She held his hand as she told him. He nodded in agreement and felt a sense of pride as to how matured his daughter has grown to be. He promised to wait outside in the car if she wanted to leave right away. Unfortunately for her, just as she was about to exit her daddy's car, she saw Roderick's parents walking towards theirs. Nathan noticed too at that moment. She then continued on to exit the car. "I'll be right here, baby." Nathan told her. She felt comfort in those words before going on to what she came to do. Not to follow Rocket's plan but to save Roderick from it.

As she walked in, she noticed him sitting all alone at one of the tables. The other kids were already dancing. Roderick was sitting and feeling sorry for himself. He waited quite a bit for her. He felt as if she had ditched him. She was not coming to the dance with him she probably only asked him to come just to embarrass him. All his negative thoughts surrounded his head and he was about to explode in tears until he felt a soft touch on his shoulder. It was her, looking so beautiful in a purple dress but she was crying. He stood up and looked into the pair of eyes of his short statured dance partner. "Why are you crying? Did you not want to come?" He asked in doubt.

"I'm sorry." She replied right before Rocket and his friends surrounded him and poured red paint all over him and hit him to the ground. Rocket, re-enacted something he watched on a movie. The whole school went silent. All Roderick could do was look into Stella's eyes. "Why?" He asked. Right before running out of the school hall and heading for his parents who were waiting for him. Nathan had noticed Roderick running out through his rear-view mirror. He got out of his car and approached Roderick and his family. "Rod, what happened?" He asked. Stan Ray came forward and stood in front of Nathan in a confronting position. "Your daughter is just as much of a bully as Rocket is." He said before turning and getting his wife and son to enter the car.

Stella ran towards daddy in tears as Stan Ray drove off. He quickly hugged his tearful daughter and led her back into the car and drove off. Rocket and his goons were caught by Ms Gomez and Mr Ray who were the chaperons for the dance. The very next day, Roderick was pulled out from the school by his parents and home-schooled. The dance was the last day Stella Marie ever got to see him again. She was heavy-laden by the whole situation. She refused to go to school the next day and called in sick. Her daddy stayed home from work for her too. They were all the other had so if they were to go through something they would do so together. Stella Marie did not hear from Rocket since the night before and honestly her concern was not on him. It was on Roderick. What he might do to himself from all the bullying. She heard that he had gotten pulled out from school immediately for home school where she never will hear from or see him again and it bothered her. It was her fault and she blamed herself. Even though daddy constantly tried to get her out of the condemnation mode she could not. She easily condemned and blamed herself for everything. It had become a habit in her and its worried daddy. What if she hurt herself because of these thoughts? One thing he never told Stella Marie was how her mother, Rosemary used to do the exact same thing but the worst part was that she used to cut herself. Especially after giving birth to Stella Marie. She suffered from depression and it was hard on him to have to take care of her and his little baby at the same time. This was not something he wanted to share and burden his little girl with. She did not need to know about her mother's battles at this point of time.

He held her head close to his chest and looked at her. "What is it daddy?" She asked him with tears still flowing down her eyes. "Nothing sweetie, I just want you to know that you are loved. Always." He held her tighter after he said that and she felt so much comfort that none of the words in her essays could ever express. Her shelter was not the home she lived in but the person she lived with, her daddy. He always knew how to reach into her deepest pain and fears and fix it within a second. He almost never failed ever. The most beautiful part was that he was always constant and constant is something you can never get all the time. People fail, but not her daddy he has never once even failed her.

Stella Marie's sick day had passed so fast and the next day had come. The next day meant that she would have to go back to school and face Rocket. She was mad at him and the fact that she got away from the teachers just because she ran out crying to her daddy, she got a free pass from getting punished. Well, technically she did not do anything at all. She was going to fix it but she was too late. Everything had been broken and not even closed to fixed. Roderick's trust in her and Nathan's friendship with Stan Ray. It was all broken because of a selfish plan that she did not even want to carry out. So unfair indeed. "*Stells*, wait up!" Rocket ran after her as she tried to walk faster upon hearing his voice. He came up in front of her and blocked her away immediately. "Are you avoiding me?" She refused to answer and just looked him in the eye.

"Can you say something?" He questioned her. "I'm tired, Rocket. I feel sick, who are you going to taunt now that Roderick is gone, me?" She looked him straight in the eye as she said it. He hugged her straight away and apologised. He apologised for putting her through this. He had a way to make her easily forgive him and it was just by his puppy dog ways. He was only eleven just imagine if they were older how much more would he do to play on her heartstrings. To her though all he did felt too genuine. Her best friend for life. They went on life as per normal after the whole incident. Though daddy told her to stay away from Rocket she could not she just could not. He continued his bullying antiques over the years. Though time changed he could not be rid of his old habits. It died hard indeed as did his father's.

# CHAPTER FOUR

---ᴄ/ᴏ/ᴏ---

## *The Rod and the Rock*

*How one is raised and the environment in
which they are raised can shape their character.
The choices that are made matters.*

Since Carter's wife and daughter left him and he had to raise
Rocket all on his own, he taught him how to be rough
and tough. That he did hence the bullying and humiliation he
caused others. Carter was constantly proud of his son's negative
accomplishments. Even after the whole incident during the dance
and Carter was called down to handle his son all he did was pat
him on the back for a good job of getting a kid out of school. The
man has no conscience whatsoever, not that he had any time for
it as he was constantly getting drunk and as much as Rocket did
not want to admit it, he had to hide from his father every time the
man came home a mess.

He would hit his son if the boy did not hide. Years and years of
playing it smart. Carter was a totally different person when he was
sober and that is a rare sight. He would only teach him how to fight
and introduce him to his friends in another term, his gang. They
were the rowdies who wreaked havoc in their little town. Teaching
your child how to be a gangster is not something a parent should
be doing, but if your mental capacity is that of Carter's that is the
best you could possibly do. For people like that they never want or
have a wish for a better life for their kids, they just have a selfish
ambition for their kids to be the losers they have decided to be.
DECISIONS and CHOICES. Something very difficult to undo
at times once done and it's not the process itself it is the person who
has the action that has a difficult time unlearning all the bad stuff

and picking up all the good. Carter's job to send his son to school was supposed to be for him to be a better person. That man never cultivated any good in the boy and just groomed him down the wrong path. From the incident that happened at school Rocket just became worst not better. He found new victims and he even hung around and learned from people in his father's gang. Skipping school until he reached High School. Fifteen years old now and all he was truly good at was fighting. He managed to make it through high school with Stella's help the only sane one present in his life. It had been years since he had seen his mother and sister.

They did not want any contact with him and as much as he did not want to admit it this really was the deepest cut that pushed him to be the person he was, no excuse but still the triggering factor of all this hidden rage. All the boy wanted was a mother's touch which he lost a long time ago so he stopped seeking for it. He had no idea how much it broke her heart to leave him. His father had left her with no choice. Missing a sister by his side also truly hurt him but all this he kept hidden deep within. His father trained him to show no emotions for people who did not deserve it and convinced him his mother and sister were in that category. Training to fight and hanging around his father's gang pushed him to be tougher. The men taught him more things that a fifteen-year-old should have probably stayed away from. He worked out and built up his physique. That way he could protect his best friend properly in high school and scare off more weaklings. He did not want to be a freshman who was a nobody he wanted to make an entrance to high school like he mattered. *Oh heck*, he did just that. This time he was not a bully at school anymore. He cleaned up pretty well but he still was up to no good. In another path he decided to take. This path evolved in its own way for the next year or so. He actually caused a kid to leave school almost four years ago what was he going to do to anyone else he felt displeased with in his life, murder them? Of course, the kid who left school because of Rocket four years ago Roderick Lee, had his own set of continued battles to face.

His mother suffered from a rare heart disease four years after he was pulled out from school. She battled it for a while and then finally passed on. Roderick and Stan Ray cremated her and threw her ashes into the clear waters of her favourite beach as it was her last wish. It broke the young boy's heart to lose so much in just four years. His mother had a pretty broken life, from a broken family to an abusive husband. The only gifts she said she was lucky to have was Stan Ray and him but she did not get enough time to spend this life with them and it was unfortunate. Death knocked on her door and took her away too soon.

As for Roderick he was stuck in the house for so many years getting private tutors that he hardly made any friends and was hoping that College would come his way faster so that Stan Ray would finally release him to lead his own path, where he does not have to be this scary nerd boy anymore not that he knew if that boy still existed in him or not because he did not get the chance to experiment with his personality in front of others.

Age caught up and time seem to be catching up faster. Life seemed to be a series of unfortunate events. Both these boys who once crossed each other's paths were now in separate paths with journeys that seem to take more losses than wins. Rocket was on a path to being a criminal by beating up people for money and basically following his father's ways, except the drinking part. Roderick walking down a path of more brokenness with the loss of his mother. He started finding dark ways to overcome his loss and sometimes forgetting that true personality of his which honestly nobody really figures out until they reach a later stage in life. No matter what he did he felt more insecure. So did Rocket every time he beat someone up, he felt so horrible, it was different from bullying as these were grown men he hit with a bat and other provided weapons. Men who had families but from rival gangs. Watching them bleed and fall almost emotionless to the ground. He started to resonate with this darkness within him. Like him and this dark personality were one from feeling bad about hitting someone to actually enjoying it as a victory. Both Roderick and Rocket experienced a wicked sense of darkness on their extremely different paths. Life has its funny way of teaching someone a lesson. In painful ways that nobody in their right mind would want to go through.

Roderick had no one except Stan Ray to lean on but it was time for him to move on to another journey. As tough as it had felt, Roderick was ready to leave home to pursue something that would bring him to a new journey to expand his horizons. It was a sad goodbye to his stepfather, Stan who was more like a blood relative all along. He managed to finish his high school studies earlier after being home schooled and got an opportunity to further his studies elsewhere so he was ready to go and live with his aunt who was living in the city.

Goodbyes are never easy but some goodbyes are for the best but of course not all are permanent. It's just for a matter of time that is required to build a new path. Stan Ray hugged his boy so tight he could hardly breathe and then he sent him on his way. As for Rocket his expanded horizon revolved around his best friend and the loyalty that they both had towards each other and though the incident that made Roderick leave school pushed them apart but it could not keep them that way. In fact, it strengthened their relationship into something more.

# CHAPTER FIVE

## *A little element of surprise*

*Sometimes surprises are not always
sweet when not appreciated*

Sweet sixteen had come and a huge birthday bash was thrown by daddy for Stella Marie. He had tried for five years since the bullying incident at the school dance to keep her away from Rocket but it had not worked it had just brought them closer and eventually to start dating. Yes, the two fell in love. They were officially boyfriend and girlfriend. So, this sweet sixteen party was supposed to be special for her, very much so that she had to have the love of her life there and daddy did not have the heart to leave him out of it. March 22nd was her day. Daddy would call it Stella Marie Day. Only at home. He got her everything she loved. Stella loved the sound of music since she was a little girl. Music on the whole was her favourite hobby. A voice of an angel is what she carried. So, her birthday party was a Sound of music themed party. It felt special and classic something he knew his little piglet loved. He waited patiently for her as did everyone else who were invited even friends from kindergarten whom she had lost touch with. He put in so much effort and all he had asked Rocket to do was to fetch her from work and bring her to the venue of the party which was three blocks away from her work place. Stella was off work almost half an hour before the party but they had waited one and half hours long.

Some of the attendees were getting tired and questioning. Nathan aka daddy was getting agitated. As time caught up everyone left one by one and the birthday girl never showed up. Nathan's excitement was demolished in a second. All he wanted to give her was the best sweet sixteenth ever. Rocket did not follow the plan but more of his concern was if she was alright so he drove around for an hour to make sure she was not hurt or stuck at work before driving back home where he believed she might have been. There she was sitting on the couch with Rocket and laughing and talking like nothing else mattered. "Rocket!" He called out in a stern voice. "Yes sir!" He replied as he stood up to face him and so did Stella. She noticed daddy's face; he had a look of displeasure plastered all over it. "Daddy what's wrong?" She asked. Just then Rocket cut in before Nathan could say anything.

"Oops, I totally forgot, your father asked me to bring you to the surprise birthday party he threw. I'm sorry sir." He pleadingly apologised. Nathan knew it was not genuine at all. "Get out of my house!" He said to him. Stella was shocked and walked towards her father. "Daddy, it's my birthday, please let him stay for a while." She begged. Nathan did not say a word to her and turned around and went to his room and shut the door. All Rocket could do was shrug his shoulders as she looked at him. She then moved on to sit with him not even a least bit concerned about her daddy's feelings. All she cared about was Rocket. She was smitten by everything he did. Even though, he got rid of the bullying habit. Well, just a little that is just because he joined a gang outside. His old man's. He dropped out of school to carry on the unethical legacy of beating people up for money outside of school. Stella Marie still stayed on as his girlfriend even though she knew he was up to no good. It was love. Really?! For someone who stuck by her all these years, why would not it be love. She continued to take care of him and give him money from her part time job earnings, whenever he ran out of his earnings. She was busy with school and work most of the time, it had gotten hard for her to spend time with daddy but she would always find time for Rocket.

Nathan sat up in his bed, looking at his wife's photo, confused as to why his daughter's response was only to the concern of Rocket's. Truth is that is what teenagers do, a father is no longer the main man in their life but a boyfriend is. This party that Rocket ruined instead of helping him with was going to be the time he lost since she started working, dating and preparing to graduate. The next step would be her growing up and moving out, thereafter getting married. Her sweet sixteen was like the last party that he believed he could throw for her.

He cried. A grown man was sitting up in his bed crying to the photo of his wife thinking about all these things that only keep tearing his relationship with his daughter. Rocket was the one in between he believed. "Rose, you would have handled this better, I can't. I can't let go of her; I still want to be in control of her life. She has to be my little piglet always." He spoke to Rosemary's photo as he cried. He turned his attention to the door, hoping she would at least come and knock. Then in frustration he opened up the door to find that the both of them were no longer at home.

He felt so empty inside when all he wanted was one thing and that was to see the surprised and happy look on his daughter's face, when she was to walk into that party and he did not get even that.

Was he losing her? Was Rocket finally taking her away from him? Sixteen, she's still a baby, his baby. He wasn't ready to let her grow up just yet. It was not fair! The first time she ever broke his heart was today. Her sweet sixteenth. Not that she did not arrive at the party that was Rocket's fault. The fact that she did not see his fault had broken his heart. Love is blind and deaf to everything around, well puppy love is. Leaving a broken-hearted man who truly loved her at home, Stella Marie was out gallivanting in the middle of the night with the man she loved.

"Daddy, seemed really hurt, why did you not remember? Did you not plan this ahead?" She asked Rocket. "Yes, it was a week ago, I just totally forgot I am truly sorry babe, I would never ever do that on purpose. I just was so happy to spend time with you and all I want to do is kiss you right now.

"That put a huge smile on her face. He leaned in to kiss her and in a second diverted her attention from the subject they were talking about. In a split second he charmed her with his charismatic words and actions. The girl was swept off her feet, just like she always was. It seemed like he had a spell on her. They continued walking after they stopped for that conversation and kiss. He then sent her to her doorstep an hour later before leaving. When she opened up the door, she saw daddy sleeping on the couch as the television was turned on. He was waiting for her to come home and slept off in between. She quickly turned off the television before taking a blanket and putting it over him. She whispered good night into his ears before heading off to shower before bed. There was still this sweetness inside of her, she rarely showed. Yes, she loved her daddy but her priorities had shifted. She was no longer the little girl who ran home crying to daddy or clinked on to him. She was growing more and more independent. Which also meant moving further away. Torn between the first man who ever loved her in this life and the first man she ever fell in love with. Daddy was the first man who loved her and taught her how to love through his relationship with her mama. They were her role models when it came to relationships up until this point. Relationship goals was one that acquired the charismatic and wise ways of her parents.

Mama and daddy had arguments and fights she never even knew about because they would never fight in front of her or show her a long face. They would never blame her for anything. That is how she saw them as. The epitome and definition of love, her parents.

The morning after her birthday, it was a Saturday so Stella Marie decided to make it up to daddy by making him some breakfast, since they both were home. Daddy woke up to a wonderful smell so he got up and sneaked up on the chef to see what was cooking. There were scrambled eggs, pancakes and his favourite bacons tossed in honey. Absolutely delicious from the scent of it. How he taught her to do it and she did do a great job at it following through. She directed her daddy to go freshen up as she prepared the cooked breakfast placing it on the dining table. They both then sat down together. She did not even touch her dish because she was so busy admiring her daddy savour the breakfast she had prepared. Which took him a while to realise before he questioned her.

"What are you looking at? We are supposed to be eating together, do you feel full just by looking at me little piglet?" He asked. "Yes daddy, that is what you used to say to me, that you felt full every time you saw me enjoy my food. Remember?" She smiled as she mentioned. He was comforted knowing that she remembered these simple little conversations they had when she was a kid. "Don't you forget it, missy." He responded to her after a while. He wished she would never forget him and would continue to be by his side as long as he lived. Sure, she was allowed to have a life but his wish was that part of that life included him. Tears streamed a little down his cheek as he pondered on that. Stella Marie, took a tissue and wiped it off his cheek. He looked happily at her and she responded by saying

"I will always wipe the tears from your eyes, you told me daddy, so will I wipe the tears from yours. Without reasoning or questioning. You told me that after mama's funeral, missing the birthday party or afternoon tea sessions does not mean I forgot you. You are my daddy; I will always love you." He leaned in to hug her and kiss her forehead. The best part of breakfast were the words she said to him. That made him feel full.

After that beautiful moment she was up and out of the house again to spend time with that...guy.

Well he had a lot of other names he had for her but he preferred not to hurt his precious girl because he loved her and she loved that dude. LOVE?

She was only sixteen what would she understand about love? Then again, he was young too when he met her mama. It felt different with the two of them. He felt like Stella was giving out more than she was receiving, like she always had. There is nothing he could have said to convince her that he was not worth it. She was sucked into this vortex. That she herself refused to pull herself out of. Daddy's fears never seemed to stop piling up. If his fears were books, he would probably own his own library. His follow up concern was always what she would probably be up to next.

She was there on her way to meet Rocket with something to eat. That guy never got tired of having a name that is constantly shot up to space and when it came to him a lot of people wished he would live up to his name and get shot up to the sky for good... riddance. Except Stella, in this case. Another day, another errand she enjoyed running for him. He had her, she always did. Though her it never concerned her whether she had him. Like she used to and she was not at all concerned.

"Rested well, babe?" She asked him and he just nodded while taking the bag of food from her hand. Then he kissed her on the lips very lightly. "Would you meet me tonight? "He asked her.

"I'm working late, if I'm not tired...maybe." She replied.

"I really want to see you. There's something we need to talk about tonight. "He said. This worried her, she was worried that he meant to breakup or maybe she was overthinking so she let it go as soon as that thought crossed her mind. After that he just walked away and she made her way to work. Her weekends were sacrificed to work and Rocket. Nothing else mattered.

Her whole day was spent on a wonder of what Rocket wanted to talk about. It worried her so much she could hardly concentrate on serving her customers. She had already received two complaints that day because she was zoning out. Thinking too much of the unnecessary and ignoring the more important things. Her manager already screamed at her twice and Fried chicken was not going to serve itself.

Finally, the night had come and she was ready to meet him even though she was too tired. "I'm bringing you out tonight, is it okay or are you too tired?" He asked after they had met. "Are you breaking up with me?" She asked. He assured that is the last thing on his mind and he brought her to his apartment. This was the first time he had ever brought her there. No one had been home, his deadbeat dad as she referred to him as, was not there. He opened up his room and brought her in, decorated with flowers and candles.

"Wow, what's the occasion? My birthday has just passed, it's over." She reminded him. He showed her a card that read 'Belated birthday present from me to you'. She was confused as to whether the present was the flowers or the candles because she loved both. Music started playing in the background and he assured her not to be afraid before he leaned in to kiss her. With a confused look on her face she let him do so. Then he started removing her jacket and next her shirt. "Stop!" She said and pulled back. "Rocket you said you would wait; I am not ready for this." She sternly put her point across. "Wait for what? We have known each other since we were kids and our friendship turned into a relationship, how long more do we have to wait?"

"If you really love me, you would, Rocket." She told him off. He was taken aback by it and asked her to leave his home straight away. She refused to leave and he then warned her if she did not go through with it then they would have to break up. She had no heart to break up with him and so she gave in that night. He promised her that she would not have to worry about anything and that this is truly what love was about. Building a bond through a romantic night is all about building love. Being naive as she was as much as she argued she gave in so quickly to his requests even if it went against her personal ethical believes. He took it away just like he takes everything else. Love is what made it easy for her to give and easy for him to take.

She went home really late after that hoping daddy was asleep but he was not. He was up watching a soccer match. He turned around and he noticed her. He quickly got up and walked towards her. Took her bag and asked her to sit down. Daddy started massaging her legs because he thought she looked really tired and that she could use one.

It felt so good. This was the man who gave more than he took. In fact, he never asked anything of her not even money. He paid for everything in the house, he provided all her needs even when she could afford it herself. He only gave. She took happily knowing he never calculated. Daddy, her provider in all things. She never lacked anything growing up not even love after the death of her mother. He always made her have her fill of all things beautiful in life that the love of a father could give. He promised to never leave her until she finds her steady wings to fly away with. Even then he promised to keep watching over her because she will always be his baby piglet. Precious as a pearl and daughter like a diamond.

She teared as she watched daddy massage her legs, she promised him she would never do anything to hurt him or anything without thinking first. That she would make the right decisions. Giving herself to Rocket so soon did not feel like the right decision but it would kill daddy if he found out.

He trusted that their relationship had not crossed any boundaries because on the day that she decided to get into a relationship with Rocket and as much as daddy did not want to agree he did base on one condition that they would wait until after marriage but that she did not. Daddy was never going to have to find out. They would keep it a secret anyway until it became an impossible secret to keep.

It had been more than a month and she was feeling a little nauseated and constantly sick. She missed her monthly mark and it started to feel really weird. She then went to see a doctor without anyone's knowledge because she wanted to make sure she was okay first before worrying daddy even more than he constantly worries for her. Doctor Prema looked at the sixteen-year-old for two seconds before telling her what was really wrong. "Ms Stella, I have to let you know this my dear you are pregnant." Stella jumped up from her chair and looked shocked as ever. "NO!" She screamed. "Daddy would kill me!" She kept chanting as she paced around the doctor's room. "What do I do?" She asked the doctor. The doctor suggested to go for an abortion which would require parental consent. She refused to do that as she did not believe in taking a child's life so she went straight to meet Rocket to tell him the news. As he opened up the door, he was so happy to see her. She had felt so sick that they hardly met and every time they did meet it was at his apartment.

"You couldn't wait until tonight?" He laughed as he asked her and leaned in to kiss her but she pushed him away. "Rocket, I'm pregnant." She said and he laughed out loud but the moment he noticed that she did not respond, he wiped the funny look off his face.

"You have to marry me; I'm not killing this baby. We could talk to our families together. Please, marry me." She begged. "Marry? Are you crazy? We are sixteen." He laughed. "You did not think about that when you prepared the bed of roses and candles because when you did so you did not care that we were sixteen! Minors! Did you now Jeffrey Luke Carter?" She used his words against him. He suddenly felt a rage of anger hit him and he pushed her against the wall. She was terrified. Her eyes widened as she looked into his. They were full of hatred and outrage, his eyes. Stella could feel heart pounding through her chest. The thought of whether he was going to hit or abuse her. Worst still strangle her was her greatest fear. She saw over the years how much stronger he had grown and how much anger he carried within. It was absolutely terrifying. The amount of damage he could cause anyone was just undeniable.

Here they were in this moment of uncertainty and here he was directly threatening her with minor violence. As she continued to look into his eyes tears started streaming down hers. "Rocket, what did you do? I told you I was pregnant and you got angry at me. Were you going to hit me?" She asked as she was crying. He did not respond his expression was cold and heartless. Just like that he changed. "You only call me ROCKET! If you call me by my full name again and show your power over me, I won't hesitate to hurt you." He threatened her before turned around and walk away. She stood there stunned and unable to move. This was the FIRST time he ever used forceful anger on her and it scared her so much.

As soon as she composed herself, she walked out the door and left in tears. Confused and afraid while carrying a growing little life inside of her. She had to keep it a secret but how could she ever from daddy, if she were to keep the baby her tummy would keep growing and there is no way to hide it. The other option to abort which would mean she would still need parental consent because she was still a minor. Stella felt stuck and lost. More confused as to why Rocket would show anger and rage to her like he did when has never done that before.

It started to rain so she ran to bus-stop to get some shelter. As much as it hurt her to see her daddy's heart being shattered, she was going to tell him the truth, but hoping she could drop out of school and get married to keep the baby. Still having hopes to marry Rocket in spite of his anger issues. She reassured herself that it was only one incident and that it might not happen again. As she opened the front door of her home to enter, she hesitated to enter thinking that daddy was home and it was best to keep away.

"Honey you are home; I have some news for you." He said but she held his hand and stopped him from continuing. "I need you to sit down, daddy, I have some news for you." She said and his facial expression changed from a happy one to a worried expression instead. "Daddy, I....I am pregnant with Rocket's baby." She came right out and said it and there was an awkward silence right after that for about two minutes as he stared in shock at her. Fear rose up in her and brokenness in him. He felt shattered at that point all these emotions in that two minutes of silence. His baby piglet who to him was still his little girl. What could he possibly respond? Would it be anger or sadness? Would it be disappointment? Both of them were as unsure as the other what the response was going to be.

"You're a baby, Stella Marie, my baby. I don't know how to feel or what to say?" He spoke out in honesty and lowered his head with eyes filled with tears. "Daddy..." She reached out her hand and held his but he pulled away and got up from sitting at the dining table and walked away right into his room and shut the door. Stella Marie bawled her eyes out and fell to the ground. From that reaction she knew that daddy was broken and disappointed. What he was going to do next was beyond her control. She was unsure of what to expect.

# CHAPTER SIX

## *Bad choices without a voice*

*Always find your voice when you are being shut out*

Being sixteen and pregnant now mixed up in an unstable relationship with both her daddy and her boyfriend just made everything feel so heavy on Stella Marie. Daddy's disappointment and Rocket's anger issues. There was no one she could talk to now because it was always the two of them that she leaned on and now both of them had a complicated relationship with her and it hurt her so much. She wanted to fix this and there was only one way out. Getting rid of the little precious life growing inside of her. She called Rocket up and told him that she was going to go ahead with the abortion and he agreed right away with no doubt about it. The next thing she had to do was give daddy a day to cool off before she got his consent. The best thing to do was to lay down and rest.

The next day as planned she approached daddy to talk to him about the decision she had come up with. She was young and did not understand that abortion is not a decision you just make in a second. It's a precious life being taken away and not given an opportunity to see the world. That was what daddy finally explained to her after he cooled off. "You made a mistake but don't let this child's life be a sacrifice made in the mix of all of this. You and Rocket need to think things through in an adulterated manner not just make a decision based on your emotions. You did things that were of an adult way so it should not be hard to think as an adult." He explained.

She started to ponder on daddy's words and if keeping the baby was a good option. What would she do if Rocket did not agree to this?

She cannot possibly raise this child on her own, but then again, she was not she had daddy. Taking a break from school though was not really very easy for her because she loved to study. So, in the turn of events Nathan and Stella called for a meeting with Rocket and his dad over at her home. When they got there all they did was ignore the points that Nathan was trying to bring across about keeping the baby and possibly giving it up for adoption or if Rocket was willing to raise his child which in turn, they disagreed for both and chose abortion.

Stella understood from daddy how this choice could lead to a lifetime of regret and condemnation because it's a choice to take an innocent and precious life that they had created. Why would anyone have a heart to kill and unborn child. If they went through the process of making that life then why wouldn't they go through with raising up that life. Clearly Rocket and his dad were not bothered about anyone else's life but their own.

"You either abort this child legally or I will find another way to get rid of it!" Carter threatened Nathan who stood up and went face to face with him. "You are not threatening me or that child's life, your son will face the consequences if you make any sudden wrong moves." Nathan responded and both men had a stare down but Stella pulled her daddy away before things got ugly. Both Rocket and his father left as quickly as they came. Nathan sat down and went into deep thoughts and Stella found it difficult to start a conversation with him so she just sat down next to him in silence. Her decision hung in the balance right there. She was not sure what daddy would decide but he seemed to be against the idea of abortion even though Rocket and his dad were all for it. Nathan expected Rocket to take responsibility but because he was a minor, he threw the responsibility of decision making into his father's hands.

"Daddy, what if he forced me to kill this child?" She boldly asked." I'll kill both of them first baby." He responded. She let out a sigh of relief and rested her head on his shoulders. She was thankful for him though he was disappointed he never turned his back on her he found ways to fight for her and make the right decisions for her. Unconditional love that is what she constantly received from daddy even though she took advantage of it in the wrong way a lot of times.

"Sweetie, we need more than just a minute to think about this, okay?" He said after getting her attention and she just responded by nodding in agreement. She trusted daddy with the decision making because her only one was to abort the child even though she was not even sure of it. Her teenage mind was all over the place and also secretly wishing mama was there to help her through together. Everything felt a bit heavy on daddy. At least that was her concern for the man who never seemed to let her down but she did that to him constantly.

# CHAPTER SEVEN

## *Growing up and growing into life*

*Remember every path you choose*
*determines your next step*

*D*addy made the decision for her to keep the pregnancy going and decide later if they were to give the baby up for adoption or raise it, even if meant without Rocket. He was not going to leave him alone though; Nathan was going to make sure Rocket contributed in some way just like he contributed to making that child. Stella Marie dropped out of school to carry on with the pregnancy. She even tried to get Rocket to marry her countless times because she was starting to feel a bond with the life growing inside of her. He on the other hand was deliberately pushing her away by avoiding her with lame excuses. So, she kept away from him just like he wanted. Like a loyal puppy though she would always go running right back to him. Crying at his feet begging for mercy. She apologised when he was the one who pushed her away. Again, she was distracted away from the one who really cared to the one she cared about.

One really hot summer day, she was outside his house waiting for him as he was not home or at least pretending not to be. She sat there for two hours after ringing the doorbell eight consecutive times. It was hot and she was thirsty and six months pregnant. He finally came back home and he was not pleased to see her there. In fact, he had a girl with him. She had blonde hair, she was slim and had sparkling blue eyes. She struggled to get up and walked towards them as they stood away from her.

"Rocket? Who is this? You asked me to come here and see you, you sent a voice message." She said. "Why don't you go home I will call you later, I have something to discuss about her father's business she is my dad's friend's daughter, Michaela." He replied. Stella Marie just glared at her before looking back into his eyes and then she left. She felt his lying and cheating in her gut. He refused to let her go but he also refused to hold on to her. She was stuck in his lack of decision making. Still carrying his child though helped to keep her quiet. It was a struggle to feel broken but care for a growing life at the same time. She still loved him and she was not going to let him go so easily.

She believed that deep down inside of him, he wanted to have this family and that he will finally realise it when the baby comes in. Maybe she was wrong, maybe she was not. Either way she chose to believe what she wanted to.

This pregnant teenage girl was emotionally, mentally and physically tired. Tired out by one guy who did nothing to ease her troubled mind but instead added on to the stress and frustration she was already going through. He did not even offer to send her back when she was carrying his child. He did not seem to be concern with her or this child one bit. Getting her into bed was that all he cared about? The things that followed did not matter at all to this boy.

Stella Marie, dragged her pregnant self to walk all the way to the bus stop to get a bus back home. She did not want to trouble daddy to give her a ride home. He would be mad at Rocket for sure if he knew what he had just done so avoiding this whole situation will be the best thing for all of them. When she reached the bus stop, she was so relieved that she finally could sit down. Tears came streaming down her face again. She was so broken she wondered if the little foetus felt it too. It's completely impossible to know that, of course.

The bus finally came after a half an hour and she dragged herself into the bus and sat down. She was still crying and her eyes were puffy and reddish. People stared at her face and some even smiled but she felt so lonely at that point. She fell asleep on the bus and of course missed her stop. She was awoken by the bus driver who was kind enough to drive her back to her stop. She went home and laid down flat on her couch. Exhausted and emotionally strained was this poor girl. What's to follow who would know? This was just absolutely depressing as it already is, she had thought to herself. She just wanted to be alone that had felt like the best thing to do. No one seemed to care except for daddy and she did not want to trouble him anyway so dealing with this depressing feeling alone was all she decided to do.

# CHAPTER EIGHT

———◦◎◦———

## *Brokenness*

*Brokenness may come but it can
build strength if you let it*

*T*he next day, daddy had to leave early for work so he offered to prepare breakfast for her but as tired as she was, she declined his offer. She decided to get up later and grab her own brunch. She did not want to stay home the whole day and wanted to take a walk by herself to the cafe nearby. So, a few hours later, she woke up and took her shower before she headed out to get some food. It was Raise Cafe, that was nearby that had the best all day breakfast sets and she just absolutely craved it. So, what she wanted she went to get it. Just before she entered the cafe, she saw two people in the cafe from the glass panel. It was Rocket and Michaela. Wasn't he supposed to be at school? What was he doing with her? They were sharing a drink, with one straw and he leaned in and kissed her on the forehead. What business was this that required affectionate moves. She stormed into the cafe and approached them.

"What is this? Why did you just kiss her forehead?" She gave him a death stare as she questioned him, totally ignoring Michaela.

"*Stell*, calm down, we were just goofing around. It was a joke she made and I just did that to try and be funny." He smiled as he responded. Stella just kept silent and stared at him and Michaela before storming out of the cafe. Rocket did not even try to stop her. He just sat back down and laughed it off together with Michaela. Insensitive is all he was. Stella walked fast and cried as she did. All she could ever do was suppress her anger and cry. She thought to herself as her mind was running, why couldn't she just give him and Michaela a smack in the face. Why could she not just let him go? Was it so hard to let go of someone who just uses another person?He always had her back that is why she could not believe that he could turn out to be so cold and insensitive so quickly, right after she confessed her pregnancy to him. It was so painful to go through this alone. When he asked her to sleep with him, he showed love and concern while promising that he would be there for her but the aftermath of it, he just gives her up in an instant and moves on to some other blonde chick who probably does not even care about him the way she does.

She has always cared about him, always will. Even when he turns his back, she would not do the same she told herself that.

Why was it so easy for him to move on? But it was tough for her to let go? Did she love him more than he loved her? Was it really love or just convenience? A pair of best friends falling in love and trying to build a relationship together. Convenient as it was it probably meant a lot to him at one point. Maybe he just did not want the responsibility because he felt he was really young. Did he think about her though about what she felt, the burden on her shoulders it was also heavy, literally.

She carried this little life inside of her and it felt so good and it felt like a burden at the same time. This child probably will bring more joy into her life but so far it has brought a lot of sadness but either way she was never going to give up this life so easily. Even if it meant losing her relationship with Rocket. She had to stand firm even though it was not easy to with him always bringing her to knees and melting at every word he says. How will she break free from this bondage she was in. This guy's ways and sweet talks keeps her constantly stuck in a very uncomfortable place. A girl should not get so easily sucked in by a guy's way of trapping her.

She went home to her daddy after hours of walking around in her brokenness. The only one who accepted her and made her feel comfort she only could find in him. Everyone else just seemed to make her feel like a burden at this point. She felt uninspired yet there was this force of strength pushing her to keep going and it was the strength of daddy's love for her. His smile and his constant reassurance made every hurt that Rocket made her feel disappear. She saw him and all she did was approach him and hug him so tight and she could feel a sense of comfort that she could not feel anywhere else at this moment. "My little piglet, are you aright, I feel something deeply cut within you through that hug." He said and responded by looking up at him in confusion. "How can you tell through a hug daddy?" She asked him back. He just smiled and rested his head on hers. "Sweetie, I love you and because I do, I feel you and everything that is hurting you I would say it is because I am your dad but that is not always true, it's only when you truly love and care for someone, you can feel their deepest and darkest wounds."

He kissed her forehead as he said that. She then got reminded of why she was upset in the first place. She was not going to tell daddy anything. She still felt like there was more she could do to fix her relationship and that was everything was going to be okay.

Daddy was excited to feed his pregnant daughter so he prepared a meal for her. They sat and ate together and had a good chat but nothing about Rocket came up because she did not want to ruin the beautiful moment and time that they had. She knew that daddy would be furious if he knew that Rocket was with another girl while his baby girl as carrying that guy's child. Scarred hearted little girl. Daddy looked at his daughter's eyes and he knew right away that there was something she was hiding but he was not going to pry it out of her but wait patiently for her to be ready to tell him herself. For a moment it went completely silent at the dining table. He realised he had to say something or it won't feel like a fun dinner anymore. So, he just brought up something funny to entertain her with. She laughed so hard and almost spit out the water she was sipping in. That's all he wanted to see her laughter and joy even if something really deep was cutting her up inside.

His main duty was to make her forget the sad feeling she carried within her. Stella was also carrying her grandchild so nothing else mattered except for her to be happy.

Stella was laughing really hard but all the suppressed emotions were slowly starting to resurface. As she laughed so hard, she started to cry. Daddy quickly left his seat and went to her hugged her as she buried her head in her hands and leaned on him. "He's with someone else, daddy. I'm carrying the child of his and he's kissing and dating someone else!" She wailed really hard and daddy could not take it he was crying too while holding her really tightly. She was broken and he felt it. He felt every tear, every heartache, everything she felt since she was little. Since he had lost his wife and she had lost her mother. She was comforted and she felt so much warmness in daddy's touch. In that brokenness she was not alone and he always reminded her of it. The love of a father that she has could be another's prayer so she embraced it. She remembered what her mother told her as her little girl what one person has could be another's prayer.

# CHAPTER NINE

## *What one has is another's prayer*

*Be thankful for what you have for what you
may not want maybe someone else's desire*

*T*his baby in her stomach that she so easily got was someone
else's prayer someone else's want. It was time for her to visit
the hospital with daddy, where she met a lady who had been
married for fifteen years and has been trying for a child ever since
but never had the opportunity. To the point they gave up but the
saddest part was that she became sick and had to have her womb
removed. Stella Marie was thankful that though the circumstances
are not right the fact that she was able to receive this child is a
blessing indeed. When she looked outside of her problems for just
a second, she could see a lot of bigger ones surrounding her. She
looked around her in the hospital it was many different people with
different personalities and different situations. This was the first
time that she opened her eyes and her heart and looked around.
This was literally the first time she felt maturity sink within her.
It's like the baby inside of her was teaching her to care for others
and not just for others to care about her. Of course, she cared for
daddy but she had a limitation when it came to caring because all
along, she seemed to prioritise Rocket first.

Doctor Lane had called her in to check on the six-month progress
of the little life growing inside of her and did a scan for her to get
to see the active little one. "I don't know if you can see this but
that is a bouncing baby boy you are having, sweetheart." Dr Lane
excitedly announced. She also reassured her that her little baby
was healthy and growing well so far and that she had nothing to
worry about. From hearing the gender reveal she felt this sudden

excitement to share it with the father of her baby even though there was a bit of friction or rather a lot going on since he started 'hanging' out with that Michaela girl. She had to keep it from daddy though if she ever went to see him because he would not approve of her even within a mile of that guy. She had to tell him somehow to maybe change his mind about this and about them as a couple. To the point he would actually change his dad's mind to be more accepting.

Tough cookies indeed they were but she had to give it a try without daddy's knowledge. After they got home, she and daddy went to take a rest. After about an hour she noticed that daddy was asleep taking an afternoon nap, so she quietly left the house and headed to Rocket's apartment hoping that he would be home. True enough, Rocket was and surprisingly, he let her in. They both spoke out the same thing at the same time. "We need to talk. No, you first. "Rocket then politely gestured to Stella to speak first." We are having a baby boy, Rocket, I hope you can give this a chance please. Look I'm sure what we have is more special than what you and Michaela have. "You're right." Rocket responds. Stella was about to speak when she realised what he had just said so she went silent allowing him to continue to speak. "I realised how much I love you and I want to be with you and I spoke to my dad and he agreed." He mentioned.

"So, does that mean you will marry me? We could raise this child together?" She asked with full hope in her heart. He looked into her eyes in silence for a while before he spoke. "We will get married Stell." That put a huge smile on her face and his too. Then he continued to speak "Only if you abort this baby." Stella Marie's smile faded on the spot. Again, her eyes were filled with tears. "No! I'm not doing that, daddy's excited with this baby and I love it, I'm growing to love him! Your son... our son." She took his right hand and placed it on her growing belly. Made him to feel that there is an actual life growing in there and they were not going to kill it especially after she met a mother who struggled for so many years just to get a kid and could not.He leaned in to kiss her and pulled back after. "We will have another chance to have a baby together in the near future. Like we would not have to wait this long. Just do this for me and I promise we will be together forever Stell darling." After he had said that she had no words to respond with she just leaned forward and kissed him again. Thereafter they sat down and talked as he offered her water to drink. She suddenly felt faint and everything went black. The next moment when she woke up, she was lying on a bed with a pool of blood and a lady was removing her baby from her, he was filled with blood and he was not even fully grown and the worst part was that he was not alive anymore.

She screamed, cried and tried to get up from the bed but she was tied down. "NO!!!! My baby boy!!! No!!! Rocket what did you do? You!"

Rocket tried to calm her down and another lady just injected her and within a second, she was sedated.She woke up and she was in a hospital bed in tears. It been quite some time since she had awoken because how then were, they able to get her to the hospital so soon. What did those weird ladies and Rocket do to her dead baby? When she opened her eyes all she saw was Rocket standing there." Where's my baby? Nurse, where's my Daddy, I want daddy!" She screamed. Rocket tried to calm her down by letting her know he called her daddy and that he was on the way. "Get lost! Daddy will kill you like you killed my baby! You monster... Get out from here now!" She kept screaming until an embarrassed Rocket left. She was in pain both physically and emotionally. She had no idea what they did and how they got her baby out. If those ladies were genuinely medically trained and how Rocket hired them to do this. He spiked her water and he watched as these ladies killed their baby. Illegally. How did he get to the hospital and what did he tell daddy?

Daddy rushed to his daughter's side in tears. "Daddy!" She screamed out. "Sweetie I was so worried. Thank God you are okay, Rocket said that he found you outside his apartment while you were unconscious and you were bleeding. I'm sorry sweetie. I'm sorry the baby is gone." He cried. She was holding him but she was angry and confused. Rocket lied to daddy and she as too afraid to tell him the truth. Daddy would totally lose it if he found out the truth. He got away with yet another lie. How scheming and deceiving can a teenager be? Then again, he has always been scheming and deceiving. She had stayed in the hospital for a week after her surgery and then she was discharged. She asked daddy if he knew what happened to the baby and he had no idea what had fully happened. He wanted to wait until she recovered before he went to see them and find out more.She had to suppress yet another set of emotions in order to protect her daddy from the truth because the truth would not set him free instead it would set him up for the worst thing imagined...death. She was going to find out the full truth herself when she fully recovered.

Sitting in front of the television all that was on it were shows with a mother holding a child and there was a rerun of the movie baby's day out where a mother is broken hearted when she has no idea where her baby had gone and she looks at other mothers with their children. Stella cried and again remembered her mother's words now it was her prayer to have her baby back while others are holding on to their baby and playing with them on television at this moment. What one has is another's prayer and also a plea to get back if it was taken away. She was never going to get back her deceased baby. It was burning butterflies in her stomach knowing that her baby was perfectly healthy and literally murdered by Rocket's or his father's sick plan. He prepared for the opportunity to do this because he had no idea, she was coming over so he was giving her choice when he asked her to abort the child but the moment, she did not agree he carried out his sick plan. It's like the little baby did not even mean anything to him.

# CHAPTER TEN

## *You have to pay the price*

*Never for a second think that one could
get away with hurting a fighter*

Stella Marie was just mourning the loss of her child as it felt surreal to get connected to this life for six months and in a second it gets ripped out of her. In just moments from sadness it turned into anger and then into remorse. How could anyone have the heart to kill an unborn child in such a horrific manner. Why would they do something like that. It was unfair and just so disgusting. That little boy was going to grow up to have a good life and he was meant to live his dreams. Living in a selfish world there is no wonder why someone would do something like that, thinking of his own selfish needs. She wanted him to pay for what he had done both him and his father. The greatest thing she could do is to tell daddy so that he could help her take action. She planned to tell him what h happened that night itself. Though she did not know the full story of what had happened because she was unconscious for the most part, the rage within her had given her the confidence to avenge the death of an innocent life and not just any life but her unborn child's life.

Nathan returned home with take away for his precious girl. He was happy and broken hearted at the same time to look at her. He had anticipated the birth of his precious grandson though it was too soon for him to be a grandpa but it seemed fate had thought so too that it was too soon. He went and sat beside her and pulled her close to him so she could rest her head on his shoulders. He loved that feeling of having her need him but he hated to see her so broken, she hardly spoke a word and all she did was lay there still on his shoulder like every part of her had just faded away. A parent's greatest fear is to see a child broken apart by the world and its way of demolishing innocence. Stealing it away slowly but surely. His tear fell upon his hand and he quickly wiped it away. His daughter was feeling numb and it was breaking him apart. He reached out his hand and held hers. She was beautiful even in her brokenness and he was not about to let her lose that beauty. He was going to pick her up. He was the first man who taught her what love is and the first man to mend her broken heart. Like a father should be to a daughter. She fell asleep and so did he.

Hours later as he was awoken from his power nap by his daughter, he realised she had reheated and prepared the take away he had bought earlier. "Come daddy, come and have a meal with me." She gestured to him. It quickly put a smile on his face to see her so happy. She was all smiles and it felt so good to see her in such a positive mode.

As they sat at the table Stella Marie suddenly went from completely silent to a chatterbox, she went on and on about her childhood and how excited she used to get when her parents brought her to the playground every *Sunday* and how after that they would go for a nice little family lunch. He quietly listened because he was just so happy that she was back to her cheery self. After their meal they watched their favourite comedy show that they loved watching together, though it was a classic and they were reruns, both Stella and Nathan loved watching a classic British sitcom Mind your language. That was her mama's favourite sitcom and always made them feel like she was watching with them and laughing along. Stella felt easily tired and again she slept off on the couch next to her daddy. He quickly went to get her a blanket and covered her after turning off the television.

He was tired too and had to work the next day so he went to catch some shut eye. Stella got up all of a sudden at night with anger and rage, she wanted to kill Rocket and that's what she constantly felt. Like killing him. It's like one moment she would feel so happy and the next she would feel like a Jason *Vorhees* in the movie Friday the 13th. Whenever Rocket appeared in her thoughts or dreams, she felt murderous. Nathan heard a loud banging sound on the wall outside and rushed out to find his daughter hitting her head continuously on the wall and he held head before the last hit with his hand before it hit the wall. He quickly pulled her close and held her tight as she cried. He knew the sudden joy she had was not fully joy but a way to cover up all the pain she was carrying inside of her. She fell to ground out of his arms as she cried.

"My baby doll, you're going to be alright." He said as he cried and choked on his own words.

The next morning when he woke up to get ready for work, he went to her room to check in on her and she was not there. He began to panic when he could not find her anywhere else.

He then received a call from Rocket who told him that Stella is threatening him outside his home and he is terrified. She had a knife with her and he was scared. Without a second wasted, Nathan left the house and hopped into his car to go pick his daughter up before things got any more out of hand. When he got there, he saw her getting hysterical and banging on Rocket's door. He approached her gently and slowly took the knife off her hands. "Come on sweetie, he is not worth it and he never was baby doll. Follow me." He called her. "Daddy he deserves to die he killed my baby!!" She screamed out. Nathan managed to calm her down and brought her away from there. "I promise you we will make him pay but in the right way." Nathan took the day off and called his lawyer friend to find out a few things in order to make Rocket and his father pay the price for what they did in the legal way. It may not bring the baby back but it will at least bring justice to the way his little life was stolen from him. It's going to take a while to set everything up but he was sure this is what was needed to be done. Even if it was going to cost him a lot of money, he was not worried about that one bit, his daughter's health and future mattered more. He was not going to let her live her life spiralling down a mental darkness haunted by this painful memory knowing that the perpetrator or both of them rather would get away with this. They were going to pay the price.

Stella Marie suffered mentally and emotionally every single day. Her thoughts haunted her. Somehow this whole situation turned into guilt within her. She started to blame herself for the baby's death and started to hurt herself vigorously. She cut herself and bled uncontrollably until one day she passed out and had to be admitted in the hospital. She worried her daddy constantly until he could not leave her alone at home because there was no way she could go to school or work anymore. He sent her to live with her aunt and cousins for a while. Her aunt always kept an eye out for her. Her cousin Mel was constantly worried about her. She remembered how they always played together when they were little. Mel saw Stella shatter every single day she lived with them. There are times she would go absolutely hysterical and do things that are totally out of this world insane. She would constantly try to go and visit Rocket but her aunt was very firm with her and stopped her. They would make sure everything was locked up so she could not run away.

Nathan would constantly call in check on her to make sure nothing like that had happened. Keeping her out of the house also gave him time to prepare everything to file a charge against Rocket.

# CHAPTER ELEVEN

## Instability in the mind

*Your mind can make you or break you*

Stella Marie always chose to be headstrong but now her mind was failing her. Depression had become her new best friend. As daddy was preparing to get Rocket charged for what he had done to his baby piglet, she herself was battling her own mind and emotions. They constantly played up and hit her at the most awkward moments. There were times she felt like she could do nothing. It ripped her apart daily. Somehow daddy was always there to pick up the pieces and she would never have to stay down. He was not just her guardian but her living guardian angel. She had her aunt and cousin but it was never the same.

She constantly saw the repetitive memory of her baby dying flash over and over again in her memory. She wanted to punch the wall every time it did. Screaming out loud only to be calmed down by daddy. She looked like a mess daily and just could not be bothered. She even had moments where she would pass by the beach and just wanted to drown herself. She was always being pulled back from the idea of it. Daddy constantly reminded her that *a warrior never quits when things get hard instead, they choose to be stronger.* She tried to live by these words, she really did but there was a war in that head of hers. One side choosing to overcome and the other wanting to succumb to defeat.

There were days she would just scream at an empty space while there were others where she would just pick up the pieces and walk on but it was never constant because memories just seem to have its way of pulling her back down into the current. Running into daddy's arms always had its warmth making her feel comforted and ready to take on anything. Her mental state did not allow her to stay in one mind but rather in two different personalities. One really strong and battle filled, the other a vulnerable little girl. It was hard for her to choose one to be. As a female the number of double roles you had to play in life is just uncountable. She wrestled with her mind constantly as to who she had to be at any given time. Consistency never seemed to want to be on her side when it came to her mind.

She struggled with being a good person and living in her guilt that never seemed to let her rest. How much did one young soul have to put up with? It's just a series of unfortunate events.Daddy was preparing her for the court case where she could finally find some justice and redeem her mind from the confusion that it has been dwelling in. Finally, Rocket and his dad will get the punishment that they deserved and she could get her peace of mind. That all depends on a simple choice and consistency of her mind being made up. Just days to the court case and daddy and their hired lawyer a good friend of his, were working on the whole testimony together. Stella Marie was required to give a total account of all the incidences leading up to this point. Whether the relations they had was consented or not. Whether the abortion of her child was legally consented as well. The abortion of course was not, it was forced and Stella Marie came clean to daddy prior to this. It was a tough situation, it would mean she was going to be sharing her most intimate information in a courtroom full of people, but it was worth it for justice to be served.

She seemed more than ready and absolutely brave, knowing that daddy was on her side and she had nothing to worry about. He always went ahead of her to protect her honour and fight for her. This time however he was unable to do so beforehand so he found ways to come through for her. Having a daddy who never gives up on you even when you don't deserve it has to be the single most important thing that one should be appreciative of. *Right?* Not when your lover appears in front of your visible sight a day before a court case. That he did! Sneakily following her down as she tried to avoid him. "I'm guessing you received the court invitation." She sarcastically spoke out as she noticed his sneakiness.

He stopped her from walking and blocked her way, giving her no way to escape from his sight. "Hear me out, please!" He begged and gave her the worst puppy dog eyes in the century. She just stared fiercely back into his eyes letting him know he does not deserve the time of her day. He started by apologising effortlessly. It felt very surreal at that point and then he got down on his knees and started seeking for absolute forgiveness. It got Stella a little embarrassed when passers-by started looking at her. She pulled him up by his hands. "Stop it! You are embarrassing me." She complained discreetly and uncomfortably. "Baby, please trust me, I never meant to hurt our child or you it was all my father's fault. If you disagree to everything that that is meant to be testified in court, I promise we will start all over again." He said then and then leaned in and kissed her on the lips, gently. It felt so genuine and it felt so good. He then caressed her cheek and pushed her back and she kissed him back. It was a passionate feeling. One that she could never deny. From there they parted ways and Stella Marie was absolutely confused. *What just happened?* He is her abuser that is what she had to remind herself. She had to put her abuser behind bars. She was not going to let him get away with this, right?

The next morning, daddy woke her up in a hurry as it was late. They had to be in the courthouse by ten and it was already nine fifteen in the morning. Daddy could drive fast so no worries there! They arrived just in time at the courthouse and were all seated. Rocket and his frowning father were there too. Everything seemed to be happening so fast that it all felt like a blur to Stella Marie. Their lawyer was speaking up for them and it happened so quickly that it was finally her turn to take the stand. Daddy had taken so much time to prep her to speak her truth. It was her truth; it was all to protect her and what had been stolen from her. That was what a father's job was to protect his child, since he was not completely able to, he found ways to fight for her justice. When she got up on that stand she froze. "Ms Stella," The lawyer called out to her but she only heard it after the third time. Questions kept coming her way and she answered them spot on until the last question her gaze caught Rocket's.

"Ms Stella, did you watch your child get illegally aborted through the consent of that young man over there?" He asked and waited patiently for her response. Everyone in that courthouse did and the next thing she did, shocked all those who supported her, especially daddy. She denied it! She denied that she did not consent to the illegal abortion and that it was all her idea because she was afraid that daddy would find out about the little life growing inside of her. Her daddy was shocked and shattered. The court dismissed Rocket on that account and did not press any further charges, as she did not consent to it and her daddy was too speechless to carry on further. He looked at her with disappointment in his eyes before he left the courtroom. It was only a matter of minutes later that a crowd surrounded someone who was laying on the ground, just outside of the courtroom. Stella rushed out to see what had happened. Daddy was laying on the ground, passed out. "DADDY!" She screamed and ran to his side. Someone had called an ambulance and within a half an hour he was rushed to the emergency ward. Rocket or his dad were nowhere to be found when the incident took place.

She sat with her lawyer as she waited anxiously to make sure that daddy was okay. Finally, Dr Rich approached them. "Ms Stella Marie." He called out to her and she responded. "Your father has suffered a stroke and is currently in a coma. We are not able to determine at this moment, how long it will go on but until then, I would like you to hope for the best and prepare for the worst." With that he tapped her on the shoulder and then told her she was able to go in and see him. She went straight and sat by his bed side. He was her provider, her everything. The love that never gave up on her and now he was completely in a vegetative state and she was unsure if he would ever come out of it. She was still studying and her part time job barely paid enough to cover daddy's medical bills or her own expenses and the house mortgage which daddy was still owing the bank. Suddenly flashes of burden just overwhelmed her and she broke down by daddy's bed side, she had requested to be left alone by daddy's lawyer. She had one choice and she chose her abuser's lies over her daddy's truth for her life. She chose to let him be free and leave herself chained to her circumstance and in turn pull her daddy down with her. She struggled within herself when she realised how much damage she had caused. She literally caused her daddy's distraught state which led him into a stroke and coma.

It was an unsure path of whether he will wake up from this and if he did, would he still accept her for who she is and after the shenanigan that she pulled. It was never going to be the same. She was going to have to step up and make ends meet full time. She had daddy's medical bills plus all his other financial commitments to carry through. School had to be left out of the equation if she had to financially cover everything else. How can the girl felt she had everything, lose everything in just an instant? It was frustrating yet that had what she had chosen it to be. At that moment looking at him on that hospital bed filled with all the tubes and not being awake, she just felt the burden. So heavy she broke down even more. She felt absolutely alone and the guy she chose to stand by over her own freedom was nowhere to be found. He disappeared in an instant.

"Daddy, please come back to me, I ruined everything! I'm sorry! I failed you and even if you don't want to forgive me it's okay, just come back to me. I just want you to sit by my side, we don't have to talk. "She paused as she was choking up her words as she bawled her eyes out. "I just need to feel you by my side. I need to know you are alright daddy." She laid her forehead down on his hand and fell asleep within seconds.

The next morning when she woke up, daddy was still in the same condition and she needed to get moving with a job application and also to leave school behind overall, well at this point. Daddy was still in a vegetative state and would not wake up. She moved around a lot looking for anyone, literally anyone who would hire her. She managed to get an opportunity within a week to help clean up a house on a daily basis. A part time housekeeper. The fact that at home she hardly did anything this would help her to hype up her cleaning skills. It was really tiring; the house was a double story home with 4 bedrooms. It didn't pay that well either maybe 7 bucks an hour but she had to take what she could get and not ask for more than she had bargained for. While she was busy with work and looking out for daddy, she still found time to search out the guy who is partially at fault for the state she was in. Everything happened so fast, she had no time to call him out on it.

# CHAPTER TWELVE

## *Love greater than guilt*

*Sometimes our decisions leave us alone
and tries to hold us down but love that
is greater than guilt keeps us going.*

*F*ive years had passed and still she never heard from Rocket again but she had no time to feel because all she could do was focus on her housekeeping job and the second job she had received over the years in a 24 hour supermarket, working the nightshift as a cashier and constantly stocking up goods. She lacked sleep and personal time but it paid the bills, it kept daddy in the nursing home. Over the course of time, daddy finally regained his consciousness but was not able to talk or walk. She would always push through to have time with him and conversations with him. He would respond just by finger movements. The nursing home and then prepared him for therapy.

She had to find a better opportunity soon because her financial stability was becoming more and more unstable. It was a real struggle and honestly, she felt so alone. She hardly had a friend to lean on. Jamie her ex-colleague from the supermarket was the only one who she could call a friend. He became her confidant and someone to always help her through with everything and anything. His girlfriend Marilynn too. Though they were there by her side during times when she needed them the most there were times she still felt so alone. Especially after she went home from her visit to daddy, the house felt so empty and so quiet. It did not feel the same. There are times she did not even want to go home and just wanted to remain at the nursing home with daddy. A house is not a home without daddy around. It was tearing her up inside every moment when she gets constant flashbacks of the court case five years ago. Now being a working, young adult the burden felt lesser because she had started her commitment really young and even education was below her highest thoughts.Her choices left her so alone and it felt so discouraging to keep moving on but she did. Her greatest strength in every situation, her daddy. Even though he cannot even speak or encourage her, he is still the reason she can keep going on.

It's not just her guilt that keeps her going, it's his love that is greater than her guilt that really keeps her going. When she looks into his eyes she never feels judged or rejected. She only feels love, compassion and forgiveness. His eyes tell her everything and it's bittersweet considering the circumstance. Time will heal all wounds and her greatest expectation of time, is that it will heal daddy. That everything she put herself through will not go to waste. The fact that he is still alive and fighting gives her hope to endure all her heavy sacrifices. If it were her in his place, the lengths he would have gone through would have been greater. That's what she constantly reminds herself. Daddy has always been a pillar of strength through every season of her life up unto this point. Even in his weakness he still is. The nurses constantly tell her that he is such a joy to take care of because he is so cooperative and he never gives them a hard time. Knowing that she can trust that daddy is well taken care of.

Sitting at home sipping her hot chocolate and crying as she does every night when she gets home helps her to release what she needs to hold back the whole day. The frustration, the loneliness, the guilt, the anger and the emptiness. The grudge that she has against rocket for ghosting her for five years after whispering empty promises to her which in turn almost led to her father's death. She felt so frustrated more at herself than him. Throwing her glass at a wall and breaking it, almost pulling out her hair every night, scratching herself and clenching her fists as she screamed at the nothingness was her routine every night.

If she never did that she would probably give up on life at this point. No! Giving up was never an option. Who would care for daddy if she did? He never gave up when Mama died. He fought for their restoration of happiness and he never even went out to find another wife. His whole concentration was his baby piglet so now he should be hers to. No guy could ever love her the way daddy has loved her. She looked like a mess when she looked in the mirror. It felt absolutely disgusting to look at her own face. "You're UGLY! You're an ugly person Stella Marie, you are such a useless piece of nothing! Why were you even born? You should have died instead of Mama! Daddy would have been happier!" She cursed reflection in the mirror and fell to the ground sobbing.

At this point she did not need anyone to remind her of her guilt, because she did a great job of that by herself. Every single day, especially when she was all alone.When a person is alone, that is when guilt and condemnation overtake them. It circulates the mind and makes one believe that they are worthless. Especially when they are not occupied with anything activities. The empty thoughts degrade them minute by minute and leave them feel utterly remorseful of their own existence. This young woman was emotionally drained and it was the moment of succumbing to her misery. Stella Marie was a mess inside trying to hold it all together on the outside.

The next morning when she woke up, she received a text from her day job employer who simply stated that she did not need to work anymore. She was even more flustered by it. Now she had to find a new employer and since she was so used to housekeeping, she decided to look for a job along the same line. Since she was out of a day job, she extended hours at the supermarket. It still was not enough to keep her financially stable but it kept her sane. Every day she was busy looking for a job and no replies came her way, alone and desperate, she became weaker and drained mentally. There were days she could not get out of bed and she had no strength to force herself out anymore. It was a blessing that daddy had paid in full for the house but his medical bills were over the top. She was too ashamed to ask for financial help from her friends but she did anyway. They were more than willing to help her. She kept away from her relatives because they judged her for what had happened five years ago. No one wanted to help her or daddy. They blamed daddy, even in his state for letting his daughter *"Loose"* is the word they used. There was no way she could show up at their doorstep.Her friends did not judge her at all and helped her at any cost now that two of them were holding good jobs and were engaged to be married. Both of them constantly helped her look for jobs and finally found one. Marilyn found a contact and handed it to Jamie to call and fortunately for Stella, he booked an interview for her. It happened to be a housekeeping job. Though she was in a weak state she dragged herself up and got ready to go. It was not an option to stay down. Stella held the resilience of her daddy in her and it was absolutely admirable *when* she used it. *Darn it!* It was way too tough getting herself ready and going through a job search process all over again.

It felt comfortable holding one for a long term that going out to find a new opportunity was too far from her mind.Torn between never giving up and wishing it all ended right now was getting her held back. Thank God for Jamie though, he was there to pull her out of *stank* that is what he called her negative mindset whenever it hit her. Well both him and Marilyn have a key to Stella's home so there was never a day she could lie to them and get away with anything they would always hunt her down because that is how much they cared for her. They were her FAM. Her family! Though Jamie had a key, he loved knocking on the door, rather slamming it open! "LET ME IN! Stell!" He screamed!

She rushed to the door and opened it and to find him laughing at her and she literally smacked him on his forehead. "I gave you a key for a reason Jaime to OPEN the door! "She smacked him on his forehead again after saying that. He just laughed at her as he entered and she just gave him a really annoyed expression. That's what best friends are for they annoy you but they love you and she really needed some fun in her life that did not involve her getting used. Now her main anxiety was revolved around her new job search and being able to secure one or her financial troubles would only get worst. Once she got ready, she and Jamie got into their car and got going. Apparently, the house they were going to, her potential employer is an extremely rich dude who lives with his dad, he is a well-known celebrity that she had no idea about. She has not watched the television in a long time or listened to any of the latest music the radio had to offer. So, to her celebrities and all the latest entertainment news did not matter at all. While they were still on their way, she was feeling really anxious. What if she does not get the job again? What if she stays indebted for a long time? It's all a really frustrating thing to have to go through again.

When they arrived at the house, they were amazed at how huge it was and how absolutely stunning it looked. It must have cost a billion dollars to build it but really that was not her main concern all she needed was to get a job. When they finally found the front door, they were greeted by Jared who happened to be the employer's best friend and personal assistant. The employer's name was Francis L. A name she had never heard of before unlike apparently everyone else she knew. When they entered the home and were led around the house to know exactly what she had to do from Jared's instructions. The job would only be confirmed upon Francis's arrival and he was apparently at an important meeting and could not make it on time. So, they spent the next hour just enjoying the absolute beauty of the house and it was also making Stella Marie very anxious because it was too huge and that would mean a lot more work than usual. Way too much to handle for her but she probably gets paid really well if she does a great job.

"Jamie, what if I can't do a great job and I get fired? What if…" Jamie interrupted Stella Marie before she continued on further. He replied her "Be not anxious for what has not happened." She just nodded her head and kept walking. She looked up and saw huge murals of a really *good-looking guy*...and his dad. *He was really tall, had nice hair and his smile was just...*Right in front of her. She froze at the sight of him. Jared then stepped forward to introduce him. "Stella Marie this is Francis, he will be your boss if you get hired... So, I'll leave you two for the interview." He then gestured to Jaime to follow him out. Jamie looked over at her and mouth the words *You will be fine.* Francis walked over to his office table and sat on the chair and then gestured for Stella Marie to sit opposite of him in age old job interview fashion. Her heart was racing and she was absolutely anxious at the sight of him for some reason that still baffles her at this point."So, why housekeeping? The public-school life didn't work out for you?" He stared right at her as he asked. She could hardly answer or open her mouth. "Are you starstruck?" He went on to ask her."I... I don't even know who you are. I just need this job to support my dad." She answered and then regretted the first part. He leaned forward and raised his left eyebrow, *even that was hot.*

She thought to herself. "I don't care if you don't know who I am but as long as I get to know who you are, we're good. I'm hiring you and you have to do whatever I say whenever I speak to you, got it?" She nodded. "You start today! Jared will introduce you to Bella whowill train you." She just nodded in agreement again to what he said. She needed the job and what he seemed like did not matter, having the job was the only thing that did. Then he got up walked towards the door and opened it before he showed her the way out. "Jamie!" She called out to her friend. Jamie made his way to her and saw a huge smile on her face. He hugged her so tight knowing it was a positive response that she had finally gotten. Jamie then had to leave due to her training requirement. So as soon as she knew it, she had to go through her first day of training with Bella who was in charge of different areas of housekeeping. Bella had worked in the house for six years since Francis gained his success. Apparently, he started out really young and now he was in his early 20s living the success he worked so hard for with the love and support of his dad. The pictures she saw of his dad hung up on the wall and the murals looked really familiar to her, it's like she's met him before but she just could not put her finger on it.

"You know, Francis is a really good son and person. He shows us respect over here even though he is so successful, he never looks down on anyone." Bella told her as they were getting to the first place of training in the absolutely huge house. Stella Marie just smiled at her and could not disagree more especially since he did not speak to her in such a humble manner during their really short interview. He basically ordered around after confirming her employment. There were countless rooms in the house and it was absolutely well kept and beautiful. It needed to be maintained on a daily basis. Stella was allocated to certain areas of the house because the lady who was working there before her got really sick and Bella had told her that Ricky gave her a huge some of money for her medical bills and allowed her to resign to rest. "You know this house is built in the memory of his mum so whatever he does he does it for her and his father. He built it according to her vision that's why he needs to keep it maintained well." Bella informed her.

# CHAPTER THIRTEEN

———◦◦◦———

## *Time to toughen up*

*The hardest situations build the toughest person*

*H*er training had been really tough because it was not simple as cleaning the smaller houses she used to clean. It felt like she was not doing a great job every time she finished the task and it was really overwhelming, before she entered her home she would just break into pieces but maybe it's just that she had not got paid yet and has not paid daddy's medical bills for 2 months and it was absolutely overwhelming and she was physically exhausted and it had only been a week into training. When she went to unlock her door, it had already seemed to be unlocked. It was probably Jamie and Marilyn inside and that it was but to her surprise, daddy was there too. "Hey, something amazing happened, some guy name Francis asked the nursing home to call us and let us know that he hired a home nurse for your dad so he does not have to stay at the home and he could stay with you." Marilyn informed her. Jamie then stepped in to inform Marilyn that Francis was Stella Marie's new boss. Just a week shy of employment and he did that for her. She was happy at the same time afraid. What if there was a catch to this? Without saying a word, she left to find a cab and go back to Francis home. Bella opened the door and asked her what she was doing back there when it was her time to go home? "I need to speak to our boss, like right now!" She insisted.

Then Bella showed her to where he was. He was at his personal gym working out and she just stomped into the gym. "Francis, why did you do that? Why did you take my dad out of the home without my consent? You surpassed me and went through my friends, how is that even possible that they did not seek my consent first? I am his daughter!" She raised her voice a little. He placed his workout equipment down and walked over to her. She moved a little because she felt oddly uncomfortable when he came close. "I know people. I am your boss and I don't care what you think. Does that answer your questions?"

He moved forward and closer to her but she could hardly make eye contact. She did not want to admit it but she was intimidated by him. "I...I make decisions for my dad. I always have since...he got sick. He's all I have." She then responded still avoiding eye contact. "Well I have made the decision that you will live in and work, five days a week. So, it's more comfortable if your dad is at home and your friends can help out." He went on... "All my employees live in on working days but only after training has been passed. You did not do a really good job though, found dust patches on my gym equipment, you live in and work five days I pay off your dad's outstanding medical bills so you can pay off the home nurse that does not cost as much as the home he is living in. Got it?" She just nodded her head again.

"Since you're here clean the gym up before you go." He said and took his gym towel and walked out. Why was he nice and yet not at the same time? See he spoke to everyone else really respectfully and laughed with them while doing good deeds for them, with her, he did good deeds but he made her feel like she was not doing a great job. Maybe because she was new, he could not be that way or someone new might take advantage. Oh well! Daddy's outstanding medical bills were paid for and she would do anything for daddy that she knew. Even put up with stuck up Francis.

She went on to start cleaning again and just felt so frail since she had not eaten for dinner. Bella noticed that and brought her a sandwich and hot chocolate. "Sweetie, I will ask if Ren, our driver could send you home." Stella refused she just decided to let Marilyn and Jamie take care of things at home so she could stay in and start the day early the next morning. Bella led her to the room where they rest usually when they stay in so she freshens up and get some fresh clothes that they had in her size. She finally laid her head down and had a good sleep. It felt like she just slept when the alarm rang. It was 6AM, time for her be awake and ready for work by 7am.

She was too tired to lift herself up but she had to. It was all for daddy. As sluggish as she felt she got herself ready but after looking at her reflection in the mirror she broke down. She looked tired and she was broken but she had to keep herself strong all this while and it all suddenly felt so overwhelming because she was so tired! Even breaking down had not been an option at this point so as quickly as she did, she forced herself back to strength. She could not afford to go through an emo phase.

Before she knew it, she was out there working and she had not even taken her breakfast. Bella offered her breakfast but she said she would have some later. As she was cleaning up the guest room, she heard a deep voice say "None of my employees are to start work without eating."

It was Francis standing next to Bella with her breakfast. "If you pass out, I'll just get them to scoop you up and throw you out!" He said. She obediently put her stuff aside and went down to eat at the kitchen. As she walked out, he just glared at her. She had been working without taking her breakfast all these years so it had been hard and it was also her first time living away from home. As soon as she finished her breakfast and she washed up to get back to work. She was stopped and requested to go to Francis's office to see him by one of the other employees. She just gently knocked on his door before entering. "You wanted to see me, sir?" She asked. He just nodded in agreement. "My father is coming back tomorrow night from his trip and I want his room to be prepared in a five-star manner. Bella will brief you on this. Everything done for him must be done perfectly. If there are any mishaps you will be dealt with! Also, since he is coming back, you can go home tomorrow night. Don't need you here." He sounded threatening. She nodded in agreement and then he gestured her to leave. *He was so intimidating, why is he only this way to me?* She wondered. Maybe it was just all in her head, maybe it was just his personality because that's what famous celebrities are like anyways. *Right?*

Bella was always there like her fairy godmother to guide her through every step of the way. She had this motherly feel that made her feel comforted when she was nervous. Whenever she even comes close to the thought of quitting, Bella reminds her that she would be fine and that there is no reason to quit. She always speaks well of Francis though that is not what Stella has been receiving from him, all the good things she says about him. *What grudge did he have against her when she hardly knew him?* Oh well, she had to brush it off and work. That she did, with careful instructions from Bella she followed through to tidy up the room and decorate it for his father's return. She looked at photos of him and his father all of it were recent pictures and murals hanging on the wall. It made her tear a bit because she hardly takes pictures with her daddy as of late and it had been frustrating. Then again if she went back into those thoughts, she would just feel depressed again.

Bella stopped her work and sat Stella down when she noticed her face had changed. "Honey, what's wrong?" She asked her. Stella just started crying and Bella just held her close. "I wish I could go back and change my decision to choose daddy over.... others." She mentioned while crying. Bella held her tighter and did not say a word.

That was all Stella needed someone to hold her when she felt so broken and all these years since daddy suffered the stroke, she could not receive this. Rocket had not been seen or heard from since the court case and though she had Jamie and Marilyn around it did not feel the same to have a parental comfort that she suddenly felt from Bella.

After that she felt so much better and they got back to work and they both felt like they did a great job on the room. Bella knew Francis's way of wanting things to be done very well so Stella was in good hands. Once the day was over, she took her shower and was ready to get some rest but not after she made sure daddy was doing fine. The home nurse they had, Rita had let Stella know that everything was fine and that daddy was in good hands. She felt slightly comforted and finally got some rest. She closed her eyes only to dream about mama and daddy, in her dream mama and daddy were so young and happy. All she was them smiling and reaching out their arms to give her a hug but then Rocket appears in the dream and pulls her away from them. He looks angry and pulls her by the hair and makes her to follow him while she cries out to mama and daddy who could not move at all. Then she wakes up with her heart beating so fast even though it was just a dream, it freaked her out. Though she was sad Rocket left her she was also glad at the same time. She managed to live her life without him in it. The dream reminded her that he took her away from them the innocence that she had, she gave it to him and that in turn dragged her away from the people she loved and it meant a lot for her to know that.

She tried to get back to sleep after that but it was really tough because her mind had already been clogged up by unnecessary thoughts. Rocket! He was that unnecessary thought. She wanted to see him and at the same time wishes she never had to see him again. He destroyed her but it only made her stronger. To know she had someone to fight for and live for and that was daddy. She needed constant reminders.

She decided to just wake up earlier and start the day much earlier than usual. She started cleaning up earlier than she should have and finally she was going to go home that night. She worked really hard to be better at her job every day and to be a better her every day. Every time she got angry and wanted to argue back with her boss, she held her tongue because she knew that this job was paying her better than her previous one. She was improving every day and that's what Bella constantly reassured her. When it was time for her to leave, she bumped into Francis who was on his way to pick his father up from the airport. "7 am tomorrow not a minute later. You are only going home because Bella requested for it. If not... there is no grace from me. Bella is your grace." With that he fiercely stared at her and left. *Why was he always so angry when he spoke to her?* Ren had picked her up and dropped her off at her neighbourhood. She decided to go to the store nearby to buy some groceries for home and as she was walking back, she was shocked by the person who was standing in front of her. It was Rocket!

She was speechless as she looked at him and that cunning smug, he had on his face. "Surprise Stell Darling! Did you miss me?" He asked and she refused to answer him, just walked past him and kept on walking. He caught up with her and cornered her. "Don't be like that baby, I've missed you!" He said to her, causing her to fume up and she then pushed him and started raising her voice at him. "Miss me? YOU LEFT! My daddy is suffering now because I chose your LIES over him! You miss me? I quit school and struggled up until now. How dare you miss me?" She could have punched him in the face but she held back. He leaned in to try and kiss her but she pushed his face with her hand and walked off. He then pulled her hair and slammed her against a wall. "You little...How dare you treat me like this?

It was easy for you to get in my bed when you were younger but now, you're acting all holier than thou? I own you! Don't forget that, especially since you believed me so easily. So, I own you! I'll be seeing you around, sweetheart." He threatened her and left. She was shaken and just punched the wall as she cried. Just as her dream was, he pulled her by the hair. He was abusive and he was *BACK!*

She was scared and at the same time she had to fight back not just for her but for daddy. She suddenly felt this rage in her that just wanted to be let loose. She slowly walked back home and she walked back into her house she had to put on a brave face and tidy her hair up. Rita greeted her as she walked in and briefed her on how daddy was doing, that he was responding really well to the medications. He had also been doing a little physiotherapy. Stella Marie went closed to daddy and kissed him on the forehead and hugged him. She could have sworn she saw him respond with a smile even though he could not react much. There was a warmth she felt as she held him. His love still felt so evident even though he could not express it. He is her family and he is always going to be. No one was going to come in between them anymore. She was older, matured and had experienced much to know how to fight and she was going to. Daddy and her work is all that mattered at this point. Nothing and no one else did. Her heart felt a little warmness at that point knowing there was improvement and that all her hard work is not going to waste.

After settling everything down she was finally able to get a shower and lay down on her bed to catch some sleep. She was absolutely tired but getting the improvements in daddy and moving forward with life really mattered more than what she felt but she did cry herself to sleep just because she was feeling overwhelmed by everything especially working for Francis who only seemed to hate her amongst everyone. All these things can really mess up a mind when you are faced with situations that add on to your ongoing stress. Most of the people her age were out there living their lives and going for holidays and prepping their future but here she was still struggling. Though she is a strong woman she's also as human as she needed to be. Sometimes she just felt like she wanted someone she could lean or help her for her and not always for all the issues she was facing.

She woke up to realise it was time for her to report back to "Stuck up" Francis's home and that became a name instilled in her head. Maybe he was just being tough on her because she was new and he wanted to toughen her up with this "tough love" sort of attitude. Rita was around so she kissed her daddy goodbye and rushed out of the house. Good thing for her Ren was waiting outside to pick her up. He drove her back to her employer's home.

There he was sitting in the living room waiting for her to serve him as usual. He could have any others to help him but he just had to give her the job, mostly.He threw a tissue on the floor on purpose and then stared at her to see if she would pick it up. *Childish!* Was the first word that came to her mind but she picked it up anyway and smiled at him. He was shocked by her smile and looked away, right after she walked away, he seemed confused as to why she was smiling and not getting worked up. It felt like a loss to him at that moment. As for Stella, after that run in with her ex psycho boyfriend, it felt like a victorious day. She actually managed to fight back... just a little. It felt good and she was not going to let anyone ruin that feeling not even *stuck up* Francis.

# CHAPTER FOURTEEN

———— ❦ ————

## *There's more to this*

*There's mystery in a person's every behaviour*

*W*hy did she smile at me just now? She is supposed to be hurt by the things I do. Francis was baffled at the thought of Stella Marie's smile at him after he tried to piss her off by purposely throwing that tissue on the floor. Why was he so affected by her calm reaction? Isn't that a dream for every employer, for his employee to submit and not be salty about things that they are to do to help out? He was surely out to torture this girl but she clearly was suddenly not affected by his behaviour but he clearly was affected by hers.

Stella walked in to his office with a cup of coffee as he was in deep thoughts and it startled him and the poor girl poured the coffee on the floor. "Did you forget to knock the door!" He screamed those words out so it did not seem like a question anymore. She smiled and apologised right away and started cleaning up the mess. "I'll bring you another coffee shortly. I'm sorry." She smiled and left after cleaning to get another cup of coffee for him. Again, he was not pleased with her being calm. Was he not affecting her? He felt defeated for an unnecessary reason.

Stella felt really confident and she was not even close to concern about Francis's reactions or "diabolical plans" to torture her. It's like she started getting used to her independence after so long. Started getting confident in working for a *narcissist* that he seems to come off as. Well her ex is a psycho that she handled just a day ago so she was sure she could handle the *narcissist*. She went back with a fresh cup of coffee. She put it on his table and gave him the preview of her 32 pearly whites before leaving the room. Her confidence can probably kill at this point but she was just trying to live her life with appreciation for the efforts she had put in.

Confidence had fallen away from her since the day she lost her baby to Rocket's lies. She didn't just lose it to death but to lies. Everything felt like it was dead the day she let that unborn child be ripped out of her. The memory haunted her daily but she had to keep going. Her confidence was slowly skyrocketing up. Everyone she worked were very comfortable to be around and she could feel that they were comfortable around her too. Of course, the constant gossip about her boss was ever so interesting.

She would hear about all his playboy stories and he had a whole book of one according to all his staff.

His dad was hardly in town all the time because he had to move around a lot for his business so Francis had way too much time on his hands when he wasn't out working. Stella just loved being around the staff, they always made her day and better and work did not have to feel like work all the time with them. She was finding her light constantly through every situation. It felt like heaven had been blessing her in the midst of the storm. People had been that broke her down but God restored her with people who built her up. She felt restored at least for the past two days. Rocket was probably around the corners lurking like a hyena but that was the least of her concerns when she was at work. Work suddenly seemed more like a blessing when she saw the things life was starting to throw at her again.

Every behaviour is birth from a reason. There was a reason why she was this way and there is definitely a reason why Francis is, well... *Francis*. She was going to figure him out in her own way as was he trying to figure her out. She always found ways to relax her mind and one of it was by helping the gardener Jimmy out. It's not a hobby of hers but she had picked up a few things from him and she decided to start helping him out a little and it was always during the time Francis had his coffee or was not around so then he would not be constantly slave driving her during these moments. She would have little time to breathe and do something that relaxes, well as long as it is something to do with taking care of the home or the people who live in it. Her concentration was very steady and sometimes she would not even hear anyone come up behind her when she was doing something new. "Did I pay you to do what I pay Jimmy for?!" She was startled by Francis's voice and fell down onto the mud. "No! I am sorry …. I" He cut her off before she could finish explaining herself. He pulled her up and did not let go of her hand, brought her directly towards where his car was parked and asked her to open the door and get in. She was confused but did as he said and he entered his car and got ready to drive. She had nothing that she could possibly ask at that moment because he definitely was not going to entertain a word she said because he looked really upset.

"You are going to follow me wherever I go today. It's shopping day for me and dad. I'm picking him up from the airport and you are my little helper since you are too free on your own and doing other people's jobs. Got it?" He asked as he looked directly in her eyes. She just nodded and obeyed.

As soon as they got to the airport she got off and fetched his dad's luggage's and placed it in the car along with the help of the airport employee. His dad greeted her as he was about to enter the car and talking to him felt familiar. She sat behind as she watched the son and father converse. He had so much respect for his father as compared to everyone else he talks to. He seemed sweet and it was quite intriguing to her. The smile that she had hardly seen on his face was ever so present. It was a picture of a beautiful relationship between a father and a child. She started to tear and quickly wiped it away. Francis had stopped the car as his dad needed to get something and prompted Stella to just stay inside with him as well. He kept staring at her from the mirror and when she caught him doing that he looked away. "What time …can I leave?" She asked him. "As soon as you tell me, why riding in a car with my dad and me is such a slave moment for you, that you have to cry? " He replied. She was very shocked that he actually noticed her tears though he was busy in conversation in front.

"No, I am allergic to dust in my eye, it gets teary after a while." As she replied to him, he turned around with an angry look. "Are you insinuating that my baby is not clean?" He questioned her. Baby of course referring to his car and to that Stella quickly denied that such was her intention. Before he could continue on his father came in with a bag of hot muffins and offered some to Stella who accepted it gratefully. "These are my son's favourite muffins, of course he bakes better ones." Stan Ray mentioned to her, with a smile. "Thank you." She said to him. It was funny how he never asked her any questions about herself and all he talked about to her was his son, who did not even turn back to her or look her way after the whole dust conversation they had. After they were done with their shopping. Francis dropped Stan Ray off at home and before Stella could exit the car he started driving off. "What...where are we going now?" She questioned.

This guy just did things as he liked, he never asked, he just did what he did. After quite a drive, she realised she was at the front of her own home. "Get out. you're here." He said. Then he threw her bag towards the backseat where she was sitting. She did as he said and made her way and then he drove off speedily. *He's unbelievable. What did I do? What is with him why do I keep trying to figure him out? STOP, Stella.* She thought to herself and she reached for her keys to open her door. When she entered, she was shocked at who was sitting in front of her dad. It was Rocket! Feeding him and taking care of him. She was furious as she stared at him. "Come out now." She gestured for him to come to the front porch of the house. He did as she said after he put the bowl down. "What are you doing in MY house?" She asked him looking like she was going to beat the living daylights out of him.

"Taking care of your dad, I asked the nurse to leave early. Told her you said it was okay. Obviously, she does not call to check." He said with a annoying smug look on his face. "Get lost!" She said to his face but he would not budge he just stayed still and smiled at her. "Don't make me scream! I'll get the neighbourhood to get you out of here." She threatened him."Why don't you make me?" He smirked as he said that. "Rather, why don't I?" A male voice said from behind. They both turn to look, it was Francis. He pulled her away and stood in front of Rocket "She asked you to leave, LEAVE!" Francis said to him and Rocket smiled at him before looking over to Stella "Bye, Stell Darling." He said as he took his leave.

"Ok, time for you to invite me in." Francis turns to her and says. "You're very forceful!" She replies as she opens her door. "Wasn't he?" Francis questions back and they both enter. She goes on to the kitchen to get him a drink and some supper When she came out she went back to hide as she noticed Francis taking care of her dad. He carried him and placed him onto the bed to lie down and then he adjusted him in to be comfortable. "There you go, sir." Francis said to her dad who as usual was not responsive. She slowly walked up behind him to offer him his supper and as she did she startled him. "Do you always creep up on people?" He asked and she just smiled and offered him the food and drink.

There was an awkward silence as he ate and she had her hot chocolate. He then stopped and looked at her for a long time and she refused to look up at him even though she felt his two pair of eyes staring at her. "Take your dad, come live at the house full time. This is an order. "He suddenly says. "There are people who can take care of him." He said and for a moment there she was shocked. Was he actually being nice to her? Or was there a catch? "Okay." She responded with no questions asked. It would keep her closer to daddy and she would never have to worry about Rocket so it was like God gave her an easy way out. He was shocked by her quick response but accepted it as it was. There was a continuous awkward silence before Stella decided to speak up. "Thank you for.." She was interrupted before she could finish. "I will send someone to pick the both of you up in the morning, pack your most important belongings and his. "She nodded in agreement and then he grabbed his stuff and got up to leave. Francis pointed at the latch on the door to remind her to lock it as he left.

She went to her father's bedside to check on him, looking so peaceful as he rested but it hurts her that she could not hear him speak any more like he used to. All she could do was lie next to him or hold his hand and he would just look at her but though he always looked like he wanted to say something, he could not speak at all. The pain was so deep inside of her and she constantly had dreams or flashbacks of the day that this tragedy had taken place. It caused her to feel guilt rushing through her constantly, even when she was nowhere in front of her sick father. Even more now she was disturbed by Rocket again and Francis her boss was being nice to her that was worse than Rocket's sudden reappearance back in her life.

What was Francis up to? The next day there was a nurse and driver out front waiting with Bella to pick her dad and her up like Francis had promised. *Dude, is a man of his word.* She thought to herself. He kept his promise intact and she had no worries at this moment in trusting him so far. The things he does and says do not always match but there must a reason he had been like that according to her perception. She gave him a little benefit of the doubt.

He did put in a little effort to take care of her dad, the night before so maybe he was not so bad after all. Her mind was so occupied with Francis that when she bumped into him, she was startled and did not know what to say and it did not help that he was wearing a suit and looking smashing. *Wait, what?* She snapped herself out of the deep thought she was in.

They both ended up staring at each other. Her neck was starting to hurt because this guy was really way too tall. "Um… can I get you anything?" She broke the awkward silence. He declined and then walked away slowly. She then quickly got back to getting daddy settled in. All this sudden change of heart and behaviour did not seem very usual and there was a reason he was being so exceptionally kind. Opening up a space for her dad to live. This really famous dude who seemed to dislike her but still, he keeps doing really nice things for her but *why?* Stella had always been really curious why people behaved the way they did especially when there was a sudden and drastic change in behaviour. This girl could multitask working and overthinking when there was no need to, *really!* It all suddenly felt so surreal to real...

It was a calming and yet fearful situation at the same time. Stella had no idea what to expect with this new change and what was behind it all. Was there really an underlining motive to Francis sudden offer? She continued on with her work after checking in on daddy who was currently well taken care of by a in house nurse. All she needed to do was concentrate on her duties towards Francis and the house and occasionally his dad Stan, who was yet again out of town. He travels ever so often and even when he is back it's like he is not even there at all. Then again, that was not her area of concern at all. She was very determined to do her best because of Francis's kind deeds and she was not going to be rude to him anymore and do her job with a proper attitude and never throw Francis any shade again. After all, he pays the salary that helps her with her current situation and needs.

# CHAPTER FIFTEEN

---

## *Always in my sight, always on my mind*

*Sometimes, when you see too much of someone
you tend to think a lot about them*

It's been a week since daddy and her moved in to Francis's home. It was finally time for some shut eye again after the long day of work and somehow it felt a little lighter and a little heavier at the same time. Working and checking in on daddy every hour because she was paranoid and not very secure with the new nurse taking care of him, even though she told herself that after a week she would calm down. Clearly, she had not calmed down not even a bit. Always telling the nurse what to do as well as reminding her of the same thing over and over again. She was truly paranoid for nothing but she had every right to be nonetheless. Daddy was always on her mind but one more person seemed to be fitting himself into her mind. Her boss! The way he looked at her made her think. The way he talked to her made her think and the way he behaved was slowly affecting her every bone. If he smiled at her, it made her feel calm. If he stared at her, she felt as if she did something wrong. If he slammed the door, she automatically had a reaction to it which made her feel, it was her fault that he was mad.

He somehow made her feel insecure without even trying to. Since she had moved in she had hardly slept well because she spent the whole night thinking and worrying unnecessarily. Her eyes glared widely at the ceiling as she forced herself to sleep but failed miserably. No one can get proper sleep when their mind is so active in the wee hours of the morning, three in the morning to be exact. *Oh Dear*

Stell! Why are you so obsessed with what Mr Francis thinks? She asked herself in her mind while tossing and turning around until she hears a loud sound outside and it worried her that it might be daddy. She quickly jumped out of bed throwing on a robe and made her way to the living room. No! It was not daddy but it was definitely a very *drunk* Francis. He just laid there on the ground near the main door and no one else had heard him come in, *apparently.*

Though she was small built compared to him, she rushed over to his side. "Please wake up! Wake up!" She tries her best to get him up so it would not be so hard for her to help him out and she did not want to disturb Bella's rest as she gets up really early in the morning as well. "Francis! It's me, Stella. What happened?" She asks him even though he was obviously unresponsive she decided to go get some water and splash it on his face and *that she does.*

Go figure she spent so much time losing sleep thinking of him and now more time wasted trying to wake this drunken boss up. After she splashed some water on him he opened up his eyes and stared right into hers. *His eyelashes were way too long for a guy and quite pretty too...* were her thoughts for two seconds straight and then she decided to snap herself out of it and pull him as she tried to. He was tall and certainly well-built so imagine the energy she had to use to get this person off the ground. He did not have a proper composure either but this pint sized Stella managed to get him off the ground and on to the expensive L shaped sofa that he owned. As she was about to get up to get him some water he held on to her hand and pulled her back, closer to him. She was absolutely freaked out at that moment and did not know how to react. She just looked right at him and he started to speak as he looked right at her. "You were nice, you know that? Then you just started being mean. Like I meant nothing. I lost my mum and I wished you had been there, but you always chose to be there for someone else. "As he said that tears rolled down his eyes. Stella just listened though in her mind she recalled that a drunk person would speak whatever is inside their heart not knowing who they are speaking to sometimes."You hurt me...so very much. How could someone so sweet become a bully? How could you damn a person you knew for someone else? How could you break someone else to please another? When you knew it was wrong. You were wrong!" He kept speaking and his face turned red and her eyes swelled up in tears as he said that. It was like she felt his pain for that moment that he spoke. After he just closed his eyes and fell asleep. She removed his shoes and put his feet up on the couch before she got a blanket to cover him. As she walked back to her room, she checked on daddy first and she cried so hard.

She felt those words Francis had said because it somehow related to her emotions towards how her actions due to her feelings for Rocket had caused daddy to be in the state he was. It broke her, it really did. Staring up at her ceiling again when she was back in her bed is all she could do. This time tears were rolling down her eyes as she somehow felt the paid Francis had been carrying. She understood the pain of losing a loved one as she had lost her mum too but what she did not understand was who it was and why that person had left him so broken because the eyes literally tells you how a person feels. The eyes does not have a voice but it speaks volumes about a person's heart. Their joys and their hurts.

Stella Marie finally got some sleep after all her thinking and then the alarm rang. *Oh my, its morning!* She groaned and dragged herself out of bed. Her daily routine had begun even before she could process that she was awake. Taking a cup of coffee to his office where was a *risen and shining! How did he do that?* She wondered. He caught her staring at him while holding his cup of coffee in her hand and gestured to her to leave it on the table. She quickly snapped out of wondering and did as he ordered. Her next important part of her daily routine was to go check on daddy before she carried on other work. Bella always bought her time so she could spend some of her first breath of the day with daddy. "Good morning, my sweetheart." She greeted him. He was looking at her now even though he could not speak, that was an improvement.

He could react with his eyes to her voice. "I am waiting for the day you call me your little piglet again. OUT LOUD!"

Stella Marie smiled at daddy as she said it. "I will get on my knees and praise the Lord! Or I'll just praise him right now, you are still here with me and now you are looking at me daddy. Next step, smile at me. I miss your smile. "As she said that she got her knees but she was in tears and she thanked God as she promised.

She could not receive physical gestures of love, like a hug or an audible word of affirmation but she felt the love of her daddy especially, every time she was around him also in everything she did he was always on her mind and in that she felt his love. The love that keeps her fighting for her life and for him. She did not just live for herself but she lived for him so she had to keep fighting every single day, because he mattered more than anyone in the world. ANYONE at all. Francis passed by and saw her in the room on her knees. As she got up and kissed daddy on the forehead she turned around and was startled to see him there and became very apologetic as she left the room. Francis just ignored her and entered the room as she left. *Why is he going in?* She was suspicious of his intentions but just decided to get back to work.

Francis raised up the automatic bed and took some medication and fed it to Nathan through the tube. The nurse was running late and Francis had taken note of his medication timings even though his own daughter had forgotten. Nathan suddenly held his hand and Francis was startled by his action. Nathan was trying to speak to him and his first try was something that started with an R...

"Mr Nate? Are you trying to say...something?" Nathan stayed still for a while and then tried to speak again. "Rod...." He managed to say. Francis was shocked and did not know how to react. Before he could continue the nurse had arrived and Francis handed over the duty to her. He had been secretly helping out behind Stella Marie's back. Or she would think more of him probably. No he did not want that. He left the room in deep thoughts not being able to process what had just happened.

# CHAPTER SIXTEEN

———— ❦ ————

## *Daddy*

*A father is meant to be a girl's first love*

*D*addy taught her love that she never knew about especially after she faced loss. Holding his hand, crying on his shoulder, leaning on his chest and hugging him. Oh the comfort it brought her is incomparable to any of the love that Rocket could have shown her and the standard of love that anyone else could love her with would not reach the extent of a girl's first love, daddy. As a teenager he held her hand and not even once was she embarrassed to be his little girl. Her mind was always filled with thoughts of daddy no matter what she did and the pain along with regret shows its little face once in a while that when she's in such deep thoughts she sometimes is unaware of what is going on around her. Worst still when her boss is creeping up on her and spot checking. As she was in deep thoughts he was clearing his throat three times till she heard it the third time around.

"Am I paying you to wipe the table off until it has no more shine left on it?" He asks a freaked out Stella who then realised that she had been wiping the same spot of the coffee table for fifteen minutes straight while her thoughts occupied her hardworking mind. She stood up and apologised three times and then went on to get something else done. Francis actually wanted to speak with her but she was too anxious to get away from him and that did not bother him at all because it had become a normal reaction from her towards him. She took a peek in on the nurse and daddy before she scooted on over to do some other work. Francis on the other hand had not seen his father for 2 weeks as Stan usually goes out to work even though he does not have to because he has a son who could support him but he hated the idea of staying home and relying on what his son had worked so hard for. His motto was if someone worked hard for it no one else should take it away from them.

Francis called his father to tell him what had happened with Nathan and asked him what he should do if that were to happen again.

Clearly his father was and always will be his confidant. "Son, do not be afraid to be there for someone even when it's hard, let your heart release forgiveness to one person at a time." His father encouraged him over the phone and he would have loved to agree to disagree but Stan always had the right way with words. Francis clearly had a lot of unsettled feelings inside of him that makes him come off as a jerk most of the time. Stan always wanted him to just move forward. He always supported him but also corrected him by reminding him that he was a grown man and he needed to move past things that he cannot control anymore. After he ended the call with his father, he called Stella to the living room. She was always fearful when he called her and had no idea why. It felt like Post Traumatic Stress Disorder (PTSD). He gave her that sort of feel whenever he was around and he had not even done anything abusive to her but it was just his presence.

He asked her to sit at the opposite couch from where he was sitting and she did as he asked. He then tried to make eye contact with her but her gaze continuously drifted away from him. She was too anxious to even catch his gaze. He cleared his throat as he stared at the unusually nervous wreck in front of him. "I need to tell you something and seeing how freaked out you are already, I don't know how much more freaked out you'll be if I told you this?" With that remark her eyes finally met his. "Are you going to fire me? I can't be fired, I need to support daddy... I..." He raised up his hand with his palm facing her to stop her from talking.

She immediately froze at that point and waited for him to speak. "NO! I am not going to fire you unless you continue being this

panicky little puppy. I was going to say that your dad spoke to me."
She was shocked at what he had said because as far as she knew,
daddy had not spoken in the longest time and of all people why
would she speak to him and not her. That really baffled her.

"Daddy has not spoken in the longest time not even to me, why
would he even say anything to...you?" She questioned. He looked
down before he looked back up to respond to her. He was not
going to tell her everything just bits and pieces. "He...mentioned
a name that is not mine but he held on to my hand. I forgot what
the name was but I believe it was a guy's name and then he did not
respond after." She quickly jumped to conclusions in her head that
it could be Rocket he had mentioned. She asked him if she could
see daddy right after the conversation they had and went on to do
so. She asked the nurse to leave as she wanted some time with him
to see if she could get him to speak.

She sat at his bedside and held on to his hand, it was warmer than
it had been for a while. She then lay her head down on his arm
gently. His presence was her comfort and strength. It restored her
daily to do whatever she had to do. "Daddy, talk to me, I need you.
I am a mess and I'm tired. I have no one to talk to, my friends are
away from me and they're busy with their own future and I don't
want to disturb them. You're the only reason why I don't feel so
alone. I'm scared. Please say something." She continues to rest on
his arm and falls asleep. Nathan's hand moves and rests on his
daughter's hand. Francis walks over to the room to go check up on
her but finds her asleep and does not wake her but stands at the
doorway as he noticed Nathan's hand on his daughter's hand. She
only wakes up an hour later to realise that his hand had moved
towards hers and she also realised that her boss had been standing
at the doorway staring at her. "I'm sorry I slept off and his hand
was not on mine but he moved his hand and placed it on mine. I'll
get back to work. " Francis stopped her from getting up. "Bella's
handled stuff. You can stay here a while more. " He said to her
and then left the room. She watched after him in surprise that he

did not scream at her or accuse of not doing her job but he let her stay with daddy.

She did not want daddy's hand to move from hers it felt so comforting. She cried as she laid her head on his hand. Her tears soaked his hand and she wiped it off with her handkerchief. His movement was very little but it was impactful. 2 hours had passed and it was time for her to get back to work and not take advantage of her boss's kindness any further. She goes straight to his room with a cup of coffee and biscuits for tea time. Francis will always be a coffee lover, he hardly drank tea.

He was not at his desk so she placed it on his table and then turned around to leave. He appeared at the doorway as she was about to leave. "I left your coffee and biscuits on the table." She pointed over as she told him again refusing eye contact. Francis held on to her hand and stopped her from leaving the room. Stella had no choice but to make eye contact. "Why…" She tried to speak but she could not because he took out money and placed it in her hands. "Go and take a walk and get some fresh air. Go get yourself something nice to eat or drink on your way. Be back in 2 hours." With that he let go of her hand and walked over to his table. Ren was waiting at the front driveway to pick her up so she got ready and hopped on. She had not gone out much since she moved in and decided that she was going to meet her friends for that 2 hours that she had been surprisingly blessed with.

When she reached her destination, the excitement they had on their faces were beyond explainable. Marilyn and Jamie were so happy to hear from her and meet up again. They hugged each other and never let go. "So what made him let you out of the cage all of a sudden?" Jamie asked her. She herself had no answer to that question it was all a blur to her, Francis's sudden kindness.

In her mind she suspected that *maybe he was terminally ill and paying his dues*. She decided to get rid of that thought because if it were true, there goes her job. There was so much for Stella and her friends to catch up on. Marilyn and Jamie were planning on starting a business in the near future and were hopeful that someday Stella would join in and build her own career away from slogging just to earn money. They wanted the best for her and it meant a lot to her to have them care so much but her main focus always shifted back to daddy. She only wanted to work hard for his well-being and all her future plans will be on hold until daddy got back on his feet. Marilyn and Jamie had to snap her back to earth while she was in deep thoughts because their catch up time was almost over. 2 hours was as fast as a minute when you are having fun with your friends but no matter how much fun she had Stella Marie's mind always went back to daddy.

As soon as she was done with her goodbyes she had to wait for Ren to come pick her up as Marilynn and Jamie wanted to give her a ride but had to leave due to strict restrictions from Francis that only Ren was allowed to give Stella a ride home, so she waited for quite some time. Ren's car finally pulled up in front of her and she got in. As they were driving forward, a car had made a sudden stop in front of Ren's car and it bumped into the other car. Ren quickly got out to take a look if there were any damages on both cars and so did the driver of the other car. They started arguing and Stella was starting to get a little scared. Everything was happening so fast and she was afraid that a fight would break out so stepped out of the car to intervene. She was annoyed by who she saw arguing with Ren. It was Rocket. "Well, well, Stell! Driving around with an old man? " He asked with a smirk on his irritating face. "He is my boss's driver and a respectable man, Jeffrey Luke Carter." She answered back. Calling him by his full name wiped the smirk off his face. She has never called him that ever. She knew he preferred his nickname Rocket. Ren was standing by her side not leaving her alone as he called the car company and his boss. Rocket kept spitting out unnecessary remarks to Stella who fury was rising within her and she slapped him really hard. "You don't get to abuse me anymore in any way. All the disgusting remarks, you can stuff it. I am not taking any more nonsense from you especially since you took everything away from me.

He was angry and pulled her by the arm and tried to choke her but Ren ran to her rescue and hit him. Rocket was too strong and hit Ren to the ground and forced Stella into his car where he tried to hurt her again and she scratched and bit him and tried to open the door that Rocket had locked behind him. Ren got up and used a thick object he found on the ground to try breaking open the car window. Shortly after the cops and a red Lamborghini arrived. It was Francis who came as soon as Ren called him and called in the cops on his way. The cops ordered Rocket to release Stella and also exit from the car or they were going to break the car door open. He was on top of her and refused to get out. Stella was literally fighting for her freedom right there. Rocket looked up and surpassing the cops he noticed Francis staring right at him.

Stella took that opportunity to kick him opened the door so that the cops could handle him after. As she crawled out of the backseat of the car the cops dragged him out and cuffed him. Francis rushed over and gave his jacket to Stella and covered her he led her back to the car and went back to Rocket. "If you ever come near any of my employees again I will legally throw you into the trash where you belong. To think someone would change after all these years is only a dream for trash like you. Rocket!" Francis said to him and as Rocket looked into his eyes, he was confused. It's like he knew him, not just from the movies, but from his past. "Roderick." Rocket blurted out. Francis kept walking and mouth the words *bye, trash* before he entered his car. Rocket was taken away by the cops along with his car. Ren waited for his car to be fixed as Francis drove Stella back home. She was crying and there was a complete and awkward silence in the car.

Francis wanted to say something but held back continuously. As soon as they reached home she ran into her room and hid herself. He asked Bella to follow after her and be with her. "Honey, Stella...

Open the door please." She knocked three times and then the door was opened for her.

Bella ran to her and hugged her tight as she cried without holding back. Francis stood at the doorway awhile looking at them before he went to his room. "I need daddy, Bella. I need him to tell me its okay."

She said as she cried and Bella hugged her even more tightly and told her that everything was going to be okay. "My world fell apart the day daddy's heart failed him and it keeps falling apart. I'm alone." She declared. Bella pulled apart from the hug and held on to her face and spoke to her.

"Honey, I'm here for you and so is someone who rushed all the way to get you back. He had a shoot and as he got the call from Ren he rescheduled to come find you guys." She then realised that she had just ignored her boss who came all the way to help her. A few minutes later she decided to go and thank him personally. She as usual brought him coffee to find a reason to go to office when she was not required to.

"You know I'm starting to think you have a desire to kill me by overdosing me with coffee." Was his response as soon as he noticed her walk in. "What? No, no I came to thank you for saving me from my ex again. I'm sorry I did not think I would bump into him again. " She said. He nodded his head and then looked back at his laptop. "Well, get back to work then." Was all he could reply to her and it felt a little cold so she left the room without saying anything. These past few days she had hardly done much work so she pushed herself harder to get things done without taking too much advantage of the kindness she had been offered. She had good colleagues as well, who always had her back even when she did not realise.

As she was going about doing her work Stan Ray had reached home and greeted her on his way to see his son. His familiarity still seems to get to her. Every single time she sees him she is not sure where she had seen him before and spent a lot time thinking about that after. Stan Ray walks directly into the office and gives his son a big hug. He knows that if he was not out or in the gym he would be busy on the laptop in his office. "Dad, are you finally park yourself home with me old man? I'm an actor but I'm home a lot more than you are. " He says to his Stan Ray who laughs it off. "Well your dad is more of an extrovert than you, I hang out with my friends not *face time* them. " His father hints. Stan Ray and Francis have a conversation about Nathan as they discuss whatever they've had to deal with thus far having him in the house. The space and the medical cost it takes to have all the really powerful equipment's which Stan Ray has also been financially helping out with. Francis being adamant about wanting to keep them in the house even though he was not stating his reason clearly to his father Stan Ray knows enough about his son and his reasons for doing things. Even though he was only his step father all these years it's like they were connected through spirit and he knew everything about him. As they were discussing, Stella was busy doing her work downstairs and checking up on daddy every few minutes.

Stella Marie heard the voice of her dad as she was close to his room and she was right, he was awake and he was calling out. She screamed for help as she saw him in that state because it scared her to see him try to speak after all this time. It had been a while since he spoke and he was speaking. The nurse heard her and rushed to his side.

"Daddy, what are you saying?" She kept asking him. "Rod...erick, where is he?" He asked while trying to catch his breath. "I want... to say sorry." He repeated that 3 times before mentioning Stan Ray's name. Stella Marie was shocked that he mentioned a person who left so long ago. "Daddy, Roderick left years ago remember?" She responded but he pointed behind her and mentioned his name again and she turned behind to see Francis and Stan Ray standing by the doorway. "Nate." Stan Ray walked over to him and held his hand to Stella's surprise. "He thinks you are someone else." She said to Stan Ray. "Hi, Stella Marie, I am your dad's friend, Stan Ray." He offers his hand to shake hers.

She shook his hand with her face still in shock as now she was sure that she knew who he was but more shocked as she turned behind to look at her boss. "Rod….you're…Roderick?" She stuttered as she came to complete realisation. "In the flesh. I'm surprised it took you this long to at least recognise my father." He smiles as he says to her. He went through a drastic change from the nerdy little boy that she used to know. She then went back to her daddy and held his hand hoping he would say her name instead of her childhood friend's name first. He smiled at her with the half smile he had to force on his face after being so numb for so long it was really too much work for him to do the things a normal finds so simple and yet does too less of in a day. The love of her life had finally started speaking even though it was not a delight to know that his first word for her to hear was the name of the guy who she helped her ex best friend or rather her ex man bully as kids that had led him to transfer out of school. Although the thought did cross her mind together with the guilt she still remained focus on daddy. It was too early for her to face Francis or Roderick as he was formerly known to her. "Daddy, I waited to hear you speak for so long and for you to get back on your feet but we'll take it a step at a time together." She reassured him. Stan Ray and Francis decided to give the father and daughter their space and left the room along with the nurse. "Piglet" Was the word his mouth to her. She was, is and always will be his little piglet. She held his hand tighter and started crying. "Yes daddy, I'm your little piglet. I've waited so long to hear you say that." She kept crying and he held gripped her hand tighter as if he never wanted to let go. It was like their second chance was coming into full circle, slowly but surely

# CHAPTER SEVENTEEN

━━━◦/◦/◦━━━

## *Time*

*Time is a gift*

*D*ays went by and Francis had hired a speech therapist to help Nathan as well as a physiotherapist to help him get back up on his feet. Not using something for too long can leave it numb and rusty our body is just like that. We need to get it back into good shape at all times and even more so if it had been left to no use. Stella had not spoken to Francis since the incident she had asked Bella to hand him his morning breakfast before he headed out for a few days straight and wisely avoided him at all cost and she took over Bella's duty instead. Also he was away filming for some time and Stan Ray had gone with him. She had no idea how she was going to face him and what she was going to say to him after finding out his true identity but she had to face him sooner or later as she's his employee. Daddy was making progress through Francis's help and that's what inspired her to work harder even though the truth was seemingly bothering her since finding out. It had been a good few days for the time she had avoiding him and working with the extra privilege of walking with daddy through his progress journey. Sooner or later though time was going to catch up to her and she would have to face Francis and talk things out. A lot was going through her mind about what she wanted to ask and what she wanted to say to him. She owed him a huge apology that probably could not cover up the damage done but he did get a blessing out of all his hardships and that was his career and seemingly perfect looks. He was not the nerd boy anymore or the bullied rather he was a bully in some way or another. He had the upper hand and she could not do anything about it well mostly because he was taking of daddy even without her asking him to. Perfect care indeed. In the meantime, she just did what she had to keep away from him but not for long.

Just as she was about to call it a day and go and say goodnight to her daddy, Francis arrives back home. Her skills of avoiding people had betrayed her at this point because he caught up to her.

"Stella Marie, stop!" He orders her and with complete and utter devastation her face she sucks it up and faces him. "Yes, boss, sir..." She responds nervously as he walks closer towards her. He stares directly at her as she looks to the ground and slowly looks back up at him and realised how close she was standing to him so she took a step back. "Are you ashamed?" He asked her and to that she went speechless more than she already was. Stella had no idea what her feelings were anymore. Everything in her had been slowly numbed by her constant issues. The only thing she could feel now was her love for daddy.

"So you knew who I was all along but you still helped my daddy and me." She replied. "If I were in your place I would have not helped me after all the things that happened." She added with tears in her eyes. Francis spoke up right after. "Being bullied can either make a person weaker or tougher as well weaker and then tougher. I broke because someone I thought was my best friend bruised me when I was just a kid. That bruise turned into hard work and success both professionally and personally. Looks like you chose the bruise over the success which equals the loser, Jeffrey Luke Carter who Rocketed to nowhere but his dad's basement. So no I don't need to revenge anyone, success is my revenge and you are my own personal slave so it's all a win." He said with a smirk. Stella Marie falls to his feet and begs for his forgiveness but he pulls her back up and lets go of her hand. "You don't need to beg for forgiveness from anyone, you need to forgive yourself first." Francis says to her and then walks away

Those words rang in her mind all night because it made sense, she had not forgiven herself. She still blames herself every single day and hurts herself without thinking. All that numbness towards others is just feelings of hatred that she redirected to herself. Time had not healed any wounds but were numbed and buried deep within her.

Every single night it creeps up on her and gives her chills which is the past that is unforgettable. The little girl who never understood the loss she had to experience, the teenage girl who never got closure or the adult who never had time for herself because she was busy taking care of things. A lot of unsettled baggage that was still heavy on her shoulders and it did not seem to leave.

Time though was often catching up with her and she was unaware of what's to come because absolutely no one is ever aware of their tomorrow. Her mind was a bullet train that never seemed to get any rest at all.

Now that daddy was getting back on track she needed to plan her next steps. There was just too much to do and the list goes on and on. Rest was never an option for her.

Time had never given her the chance to slow down it always kept her moving and the clock always failed her because the moment she finally got to rest, her alarm would scream for her to wake up. The days just kept moving and Stella Marie had to move along with it. Her daddy was talking to her daily slowly but surely he was reaching the heights he was expected to reach by all who were rooting for his complete recovery. Stella Marie and daddy were not alone in this journey, they had a whole estate of people willing to walk with them through this journey. She felt the love at the same time she carried guilt inside of her. It was a battle of acceptance and rejection within her constantly. She could literally imagine herself in a ring with herself.

It felt good looking at daddy having all the support and love around him. Then she looked back at the people who were the main supporters and the guilt overwhelmed her because every time she looked at them, she saw the face of a little broken boy and an angry father who had carried the hurt along with his son all those years ago.

Even though time seemed to have heal them in some ways, it had not completely healed her or rather not at all.

Furthermore, looking at daddy's recovery gave her flashbacks from when he first passed out, just outside the courtroom where she took Rocket's side. It was all a mashup that she did not want to have in the playlist of her mind but it played on repeat and it was draining. Completely and utterly draining. Daddy was watching her think as hard as she worked and called her towards him. He could sense the restlessness in her and the lack of focus on what she was actually doing.

She left what she was doing and went over to him. "My lit..tle Piglet." He said stammering. "Let go." Was all that he said and held her hand. He was the second person in 2 days pretty much telling her to move on. To stop harping on things in her mind that should have been long-gone. It was taking up most of the energy inside of her and breaking her down. If she broke down anymore she would be less productive at work and her boss is not the kind who would keep someone who was less productive. Everything revolved around time. Healing, productivity, satisfaction, confidence, resolution all of this revolved around time.

Daddy's recovery also revolved around time and it was faster than expected on some days and some days it just fluctuated. There were things she had to get used to now that he was not just lying still on a bed. He was moving around and it meant that the nurse had to be extra careful with him because he was so fragile and even a slight fall could do extreme damage and slow down the progress that had been made so far. We fail to recognise that someone waking up from tragic situations are just step 1 of progress there are many more stages to follow and it can be a lot more strenuous than it may seem. She was anxious every time the nurse brought him out for a walk and handled him. Her heart pounded in fear and restlessness overtook her. She had to find peace and rest which was quite the struggle. Daddy was also struggling through his recovery there were good days and bad days. He was tough and a fighter. It took him so long to get up but he did. He took him so long to talk, but he did. Everything he did took time but it had results.

It was a beautiful journey of restoration in the most difficult moments. Restoration and change is an ongoing journey that involves time and that we all have to face in our lives in order to be humbled and move forward in life with one's head held high. In order to get there our head had to be lowered first. The moments that Stella Marie and daddy had to face all these years were moments that lowered their heads so much. Watching daddy inspired her to get stronger and away from *all* the thoughts and feelings that has kept her so down every time the day ended. She finally got to have a sit down with daddy outside and have a chat with him. The weather was beautiful it was cool and sunny at the same time. "Stella." He struggled to say but he forced it anyway. "Compassion....is the most understood language, but the least used." He said through his speech deficiency. She looked at him with no response at the back of her mind. She waited to hear from him more as it has been a long time since she had heard from him. A very long time. "You, use a lot. I'm. Proud of you." He spoke with little pauses in between. She teared as he said that. Daddy was proud of her and it made her feel so reassured. She laid her head on his shoulder, gently and felt so comforted. A comfort she had longed for since she almost lost him.

Time was a gift that she wanted to hold on to dearly because it made her feel that she finally had a sense of how it heals but it was healing daddy really well but her emotional state was absolutely wounded and that would take a lot of downloading of unnecessary baggage to completely heal of. Does anyone really get completely healed of emotional wounds that had been left by deep cuts in this lifetime? That really depended on the person themselves and two words that daddy said to her *Let Go*. These were words that she needed to create a reality out of. Her wounds were a subject of her emotional hoarding that time had allowed to build inside of her. Time can heal what time had also build. It was time to break down the walls but sometimes it was not easy to do it on your own because when you are on your own you usually build more walls than you break down. Lucky or rather more unlucky was the fact that she had a grumpy boss to that for her daily. He challenged her pride every single day and he crushed it to make sure she had none left at all. Well at least that was what she thought he was doing.

Bella never ceased to be ever present for her under every circumstance and she loved working with her because it did not feel so lonely to have face each day. She looked back for a moment and started counting her blessings that she was not actually lacking emotional support, there were people around her and it made things feel lighter even though it was extremely heavy. Life was tough but no one has to face it alone even though at times one is left alone to face certain situations. It's okay to also seek help and reach out to people who would be willing to help. She and Bella built a beautiful bond with each other and it was beautiful. Growing up with no female figure after the death of her mama it had been so long till she had found someone like Bella who had the motherly touch that she had lacked. Bella raised two children who were now grown up and though they have asked her to stop working for Francis which she refused to. She loved her independence since she was already since young and furthermore being a single mum. To her, Francis was like a son and she could never leave him and now since getting to know Stella Marie she took her under her wings like she were her own daughter.

Francis has been away again for a shoot so it was less stressful for her also she had no one to be intimidated around so that felt really good too. The days seemed to be moving fast even though he was not around because she was just busy with work and daddy that she did not even have time to focus on her emotional rollercoaster as she was too tired to stay awake. There was so much more efforts required from her and energy that made her more exhausted. As soon as she laid her head down to rest the next thing she hears is her alarm and that would mean she has had at least 6 hours of sleep compared to the previous weeks where she suffered those mental breakdowns. Time was moving really fast and it felt like a relief. She had a big goal to see daddy in full circle recovery sooner than the doctor had advised and that would take a lot of hard work from him, the nurse and her. Sacrifice leads to success. Daddy struggled but persevered astonishingly. Every time he saw his daughter he pushed himself even harder to improve and he did. They were and always will be each other's rock most definitely. She sacrificed for him because he first sacrificed for her. She worked hard for him because he first worked hard for her and now he is doing the same back, working hard for her.

Through selflessness and love both father and daughter have carried each other through spiritually. Time only proved it even more through each circumstance that they had to face together and individually. Not many children had the privilege of this kind of father daughter relationship. It was a blessing to have it.

Daddy and Stella had beautiful conversations every day and it was what she lived for and it helped her. Her spirit felt uplifted just by the simple words that daddy spoke to her and it was a relief. They were reaching their full and complete breakthrough. Finally, it was a strong hope that Stella Marie had carried deep within her. Life had not been fair thus far and it has been quite a journey of stress and shame for a young girl to shoulder. Having to grow up so fast in her youth and becoming a breadwinner also in her youth. When some of the friends she knew were getting their college degrees and she could not continue her studies. There was just too much for her to handle and getting her baby removed from her and watching it die has been a complete nightmare for so long. It had never left her mind knowing her child's life was stripped away by the selfishness of someone else. It was a bond that was broken way too soon. Daddy saw his daughter in deep thoughts and tears as she was cleaning her room.

It was very sudden flashback that popped up in her mind while she was trying to get her work done. He sat up in his bed and called his daughter to come closer to him.

"Sit here, little piglet. I forgive you. Please forgive yourself. Stop blaming yourself and letting these thoughts overtake you. What happened, happened. You can't go back and you can't change the past but you can change tomorrow. The only way is not to carry your past with you but to bury what does not need to be brought forward." He put his hand on hers as he said that and she felt better.

# CHAPTER EIGHTEEN

———— ⁜ ————

## What our eyes see and speak

*The eye is the lamp of the body*

$\mathcal{W}$hat the eye sees is very important especially if it does not see the right thing it will end up releasing negativity to the heart and affecting the whole way a person feels and thinks. Especially a child, what they are exposed to when young can affect a lot of how they react to things growing up until they are properly learned towards what they see and experience in life. Again the eye is the lamp of the body and if it is healthy the whole body will be full of light but if your eyes are unhealthy, your whole body will be full of darkness. That is what her daddy read from the bible to her and reminded her how important it is to always seek the positivity of any situation. If she focused on the dark things in life only darkness will fill her completely. He knew that his little girl had experienced much pain and rejection at such a young age and it broke him every time he looked in her eyes because he saw the pain. Her eyes always told a story and when she was filled with joy it was lit up but when she recalled pain or felt it her eyes spoke clearly, very clearly. Daddy still knew every bit of her and she could not fool him even one bit.

Her moments of breaking in secret and silence still was very obvious to him. She was shattered deep inside and could not see that the fight she had was within herself. She often found every pain of someone else very visible but not her own. Her battle was too invisible to her until she was all alone and it hurt like hell. Her eyes spoke it but she never saw it and that's because she hardly looked in the mirror. It did not catch her attention that she needed help she always saw others and not her. Someone other than daddy though constantly watched her and it got her up on the anxiety scale because it was her boss. She always felt like she was not doing a great job when he watched her and it drove her fear level up really high. There was no freedom to breathe when she saw him though all he did was look. He had no complaints and said nothing at all but to her his eyes were judging her. *ALWAYS.*

Giving him coffee was like climbing a mountain for her and it was a lot of work to get up there and give him his coffee without feeling like she messed up. He asked her to sit down every time he needed to talk and today was another day she had to hear him talk again. "I want you to follow me to a premier." She was surprised. "To help me carry stuff." Her reaction went back to normal after that. "Okay." She replied. After that he got up and went to get a big bag with something inside and passed it to her and she wondered if it was the stuff she was going to be carrying but then he asked her to open it up and take out what was inside. It was a beautiful emerald green dress that she absolutely loved. "You would have to wear this to the premiere. I have someone who would do your makeup and getting ready. I would get a professional but I think you'd feel more comfortable with Bella."

She agreed to it and then got up to leave as he instructed her to. She was smiling outside his door as she closed it. She was going for a movie premier and it was too surreal for her it did not matter if she were going there to be his domestic help she was going to wear a beautiful dress and wonderful makeup on to be the help. She ran to tell daddy the good news but he was asleep so she ran into Bella who already knew. Bella hugged her and then smiled as she could see the joy in Stella's eyes it was full of light like she had won an award or something. She finally got to dress up and go somewhere and that was for a movie premiere. It was a once in a lifetime chance and she was over the top.

She felt so uplifted to work harder after this and it made her feel even better at this moment. She always needed a little encouragement and the anxiety she felt just left her knowing that he is not actually disappointed in her like he usually looks. Yes, his look can be really intimidating but it was not how it looked like as far as she found out, *right?* That whole night the excitement got the best of her and she could not sleep she was beyond excited. How can a girl who created such a mess of her life still get so much beautiful graciousness to get opportunities that she did. It's like heaven still gave her everything in spite of losing everything. It was not what she lost but it was what she needed.

Her daddy being taken care of until he recovered and also being able to live in such a big and beautiful home. Having people care for him while she works and still being able to go out with her friends.

She was finally pondering on the goodness in her life and not the pain. She was thanking God for the benefits that she has received in spite of all she had done. This too from the person she had hurt so deep that he had left the school. As adults looking back at it, did not seem like such a dire situation but as a child it would have been so painful for him.

It was still something that he carried within him. Being bullied can be a scar even though it is also a vessel of pushing one to be stronger.

Francis still did good things for her that she clearly did not deserve from him. He still had the thrill of her being his "servant" in the midst of all his kindness. He clearly got a kick out of it. She was too busy thinking but this time not with tears in her eyes with a smile on her face. Well that smile would soon fade when the alarm starts to ring she thought to herself so she forced herself to sleep. It did ring just a couple of hours after she slept. She jumped out of bed and rushed to get ready hoping that she will not be late to get her work done as she had to get ready early in the evening to go to the premier so that would mean she would have to get all her work completed earlier. She did it in excitement and surprisingly with less anxiety as there were positive vibes everywhere all of a sudden. Bella had noticed the joy in her while she was doing her own work. She had so much love for Stella and seeing her happy was one of the things that made her happy too. Now she was going to be her fairy godmother for the premiere.

Time was moving so fast because she was working so hard and though she was tired she felt accomplished enough for the day. Well, before she knew it she was sitting in front of the mirror and getting ready for the event. Feeling like a teenager getting ready for prom. Bella was her fairy godmother who was working her magic on her. "Honey, you are very nervous, it shows clearly on your face." Bella noted to her as she was doing up her hair and makeup.

"I'm excited but I am also scared that whatever I need to do, I am going to mess up and he's gonna be mad at me and make a scene or something in front of all those big time people who don't even know I exist." Stella replied her. Bella put down her things and went in front of Stella and put both her hands on both Stella's shoulders in a reassuring manner. "You have not even stepped out of this room or house and you are already doubting yourself. The person who needs to be confident in you the most, is not me, is not Francis and it's not your dad. It's you, honey. You need to trust you. If you trust you the way God trusted you enough to give you these blessings, then you're gonna be perfect." Bella said to her and as soon as she noticed the tears in her eyes she gently wiped it off. Her touch was the touch of a mother that Stella had not received in years. The amazing thing is Bella has been that mother figure to Francis as well. So you could say she was a mother figure to the motherless. An awesome one at it. She continued to get her ready for the event.

She was done almost one and half hours later and just in time for them to leave. Francis was already waiting in the car so she had to take her leave as quick as possible but first she went to say goodbye to daddy. He was sitting up on his bed and as soon as he saw her, his jaw dropped and he teared. "My princess is dressed as princess. You're so beautiful just like your mama. Even more so.

"He said to her and she rushed to hug him. After that they saw Ren waiting outside the room door signing to her that they had to leave. So when she rushed down to the driveway Ren opened the car door for her and led her in to the backseat and at the front was a beautiful sight to see. It was Francis in a tux and he looked absolutely stunning with his hair up.

He looked at her from the mirror and for a long time in fact. "I'm glad you arrived as soon as you decided to." He commented sarcastically and then drifted his sight somewhere else. His comment did not seem to bother her at all she just smiled and ignored his mood.Once they arrived at the location there was actually a red carpet and he exited from the car while she did her duty and collected his items to be carried for him. He asked her to stay close to him and not to wander off on her own because he noticed how excited she was.

There were lights everywhere and she stayed far from him yet close because she did not want to get in the way or for anyone to get any wrong ideas. The whole time all she could notice was her boss glancing behind every few moments looking for her well because she was holding all his belongings and he did not want her to lose it, *Right?* She thought to herself. There was not even a moment he missed looking back even if it were in ten minute intervals. It kind of made her more nervous and almost drop things along the way but she managed to save it.

When they were inside the theaterette, he made her to sit next to him until the movie ended. Not once did he disturb her for anything. She had the opportunity to enjoy the movie and his acting skills until the end. It felt a little bit odd though to her that he did not even ask her for anything because she came as his assistant so that would mean she would need to do things for him. He even had the server give her food and drinks and not ask her to help him get anything. Once the premier ended he made sure Ren had picked her up so that he could stay for the afterparty which he did not ask her to stay for. His excuse was that he did not need her services anymore.

As she sat in the car she started questioning her purpose for attending the premier, when she had done nothing at all but basically enjoy the event. It moved so quickly she did not even feel like she went anywhere or did anything.

Ren noticed that she was deep in thought. "Are you okay, Stella?" He asked out of concern. She replied with a nod stating that she was. Her main aim was to speak to Bella the next day because it was really late and she might already be in bed. Ren decided to question her again. "I know there is something bothering you, did Francis say anything to hurt you? Was he mean to you? "She then sat up straight to respond. "No he was not, he was nice to me. I thought he wanted me to come here to be of assistance to him but he allowed me to enjoy the event without even asking me to do anything and got the server to serve us food instead of me serving him.

I'm just baffled by this that is all." Ren then stopped the car to turn around and speak to her. "You thought he brought you to this premier to work?" She nodded in agreement. He then said to her "He wanted you to take a break that's why he brought you here. So that you would be able to dress up and watch a nice movie and feel like a celebrity for one day in your life. He only asked you to carry those things because he did not want you to know this." Ren said to her and immediately she teared. It was definitely tears of joy and she felt like speaking to him but Ren made it clear he did not want her to know his positive and pure intention.

When she reached home she went to check on daddy who was already fast asleep and snoring before she headed to freshen up but she did not go to bed. She decided to wait up for her boss no matter how late it was. Her plan was to thank him for letting her go to the premier with him and not to make it obvious that she knew his intentions from her conversation with Ren. She waited and waited. Still waited until it was already 6 am in the morning but she was not giving up. He might come home drunk and she might still need to take care of his drunken state as she did before. She was pretty sure he could not hold his alcohol and that these after parties served way too much of it. Her thoughts were constant on him. It was pure gratitude for the great thing he had done for her to just have a break. No one other than daddy would do anything like that for her not even Rocket. In fact Rocket took a lot from her and did not give her much in return but she still loved him.

One thing about Stella Marie was that she had a lot of gratitude inside of her and she always held a decency to show it to people who did right by her. At this point Francis A.K.A Roderick had done so much good for her in spite of the fact that she had bullied him for the sake of Rocket back when they were younger. She started recalling their friendship. The strong friendship that both their dads had with each other had kindled a friendship between the two kids. Due to the bullying incident, Nathan and Stay Ray had a falling out for years until this point where Nathan and Stella had moved in to Francis's home.

Clearly, Stan Ray had no hard feelings towards Nathan or Stella seeing as to how he supported his son's decision to help them out even if it meant going out of his way to do so. All his son had to do to convince him was just a look of reassurance.

Not much words were involved. With such goodness that she received from these people she had nothing but complete and utter respect for them at this point. All the things they did that she clearly did not deserve from them. Totally unmerited favours received from this wonderful family. She could not be more grateful and the easiest way for her to be grateful was to be submissive and do what her boss says without arguing even if he was not on his best mood. It was already 7 am when she hear the door unlock and rushed out to see if he had returned and he did but with a girl. So she went back inside her room and hid herself. She felt uncomfortable all of a sudden. She did not know why so she just brushed it off. It was already time for her to wake up but she had not slept at all. She quickly went to get ready to get to work since the boss was home. Just in time as she was about to leave her room, she opened the door to see Francis standing outside ready to knock on her door and they both were startled by each other. "I have a guest, Agnes and both of us would love to have some coffee please." He said and that walked over to the living room after she agreed to prepare his coffee. Bella was outside doing some work so Stella made her way to the kitchen to prepare some coffee for them.

She even prepared some breakfast for them even though he did not ask but she thought and it was only mandatory to go the extra mile sometimes that is a quality of an excellent worker. When she made her way to serve them for some reason she could not face Rita and looked down all the way until Francis called her back. He then introduced her to Rita officially. "This is Agnes, my cousin, she's going to be living here for a bit. So you are too assist her with anything she needs." Stella nodded in agreement and noticed a bruise on Rita's arm as her eyes wandered. Then she looked back into Rita's eyes and though she was smiling there was an inch of sadness in her eyes and it seemed familiar to Stella.

She smiled and introduced herself before offering to get her anything else. Then she declined so Stella left her side and went to carry out her duties. Agnes looked at her cousin with a huge smile on her face and he then threw the cushion at her. Stella noticed that as she was about to walk back to over to ask him something else but noticed them doing that and decided not to. Bella walked into the kitchen and found her daydreaming a little so she gave her a little scare and she dropped the pan she was holding on the floor.

"I'm guessing you did not sleep last night due to the aftermath of your celebrity life excitement." Bella joked. Stella gave her smiled at her as she picked up the pan. "Did you meet Rita? She is one of the sweetest girls ever and also Francis's favourite cousin because she looks exactly like his mother when she was younger. Her mother is his mother's twin and Rita is the spitting image of her mum." She explained to her. Stella also reacted with a smile. "Is she married or single?" Stella asked and Bella looked at her for awhile before responding. "She's engaged to a really rich guy and they've been dating since high school. She loves him very much and would do anything for him." Stella nodded her head and continued her work but at the back of her mind the bruise on Rita's arm bothered her but she did not want to start a gossip based on just assumptions so she just quietly continued her work. "Honey, you are bothered by something." Bella called her out on it. Then Stella looked up at her. Her eyes spoke clearly for Bella to understand just as Agnes eyes spoke to her.

When she went back to the living room just to clean up after them she noticed Agnes sitting alone and asked her where Francis was and he had gone to take a shower. "Would you like anything else Agnes?" She asked. "No thanks, I'm just gonna get some rest in the guest room." She replied and Stella offered to show her where it is. She even helped to carry Agnes's luggage even though Agnes did not want to trouble her. She felt a need to reach out to her even though earlier she might have caught a certain unsettled feeling of jealousy because she assumed Agnes was Francis girlfriend and she clearly she was confused why she even caught that. As she placed the bags down in the guest room she turned around and looked Agnes in the eye and reassured her. "If you need anything, anything at all Agnes, please do not hesitate to come to me."

When she said that Agnes face lit up with a beautiful smile and she walked over and hugged her.

Stella did not know how to respond at first and then hugged her back. She was quite shocked at her reaction. They barely even knew each other and when they pulled apart she saw tears in her eyes. Stella wanted to speak to her but just at the moment Francis showed up at the doorway and Stella quickly left the room. There was a lot of pain in this girl and as she hugged her she felt it and her eyes said a thousand words. It lit up with joy when she reassured her and it expressed pain when she pulled apart from the hug.

Stella was afraid to try to reach out to Agnes because that would absolutely be crossing the boundaries as an employee of her cousin. Then suddenly her thoughts overpowered her *How can someone who is broken herself reach out to another broken vessel?* That thought was loud and clear until it snapped her back to reali*t*y. It felt painful listening to that so to calm her mind she went to the one person who she knew understood her the most. Daddy sat up in joy as he saw his little piglet walk towards him. "Good day my sweet little girl." He said she came over to hug him and rest by his side. "You are looking more and more like your mama, as beautiful as ever." She kissed him on the forehead after he said that and she teared. He reminded her of her strength every time she went to him. It was for him that she had to be strong and it was for him that she had to move on from her past. Every time she looked at his eyes light up her heart felt warmth she could never explain. Not many girls, she reminded herself have the precious love of a daddy as she does. Who came back to life just for her not giving in to the death that was waiting for him.

There was another force that pushed her to work harder and that was her boss's ever present presence whenever she took a little break. He was right at the doorway so she quickly kissed daddy again and proceeded to leave the room but Francis held her back. "I need to talk to you. Follow me to the garden." She was worried at the way he looked at her and the way he said it. Something was not right and it worried her. When they went to the garden Bella was there too sitting and waiting for them. "Stell, you might want to sit next to me." Bella called out to her and she did as she said.

Francis sat at the opposite chair and looked at Stella intensely. "We spoke to the doctor who checked on your dad yesterday while we were at the event and he actually wanted to speak to you. I insisted that he tell me what was the concern paid him to do it." Stella sat up in discomfort she was worried of what was going to be said. "Your dad is not doing as well as he looks. He got better from the stroke but he has been hit by colon cancer. It was growing in him and he felt a little pain and he couldn't bear it. So I had to take you out yesterday so the scan could be done. He'll be going for chemo but his body is too weak to take in too much treatment. So the doctor suggested to do an operation to remove the cancer growth but there would only be a 20 percent chance that he would survive it. Or to keep him comfortable for the next 2 months that he has left. He does not want the operation, he wants to live happily for these 2 months. I'm sorry it had to be behind your back." Tears streamed down her face it is like her joy never had a long life it was always short lived. "God does not like me to be happy does he? I just get karma after karma. I just got him back and how could I have to lose him. It's been years he wasn't conscious and only weeks since i've got him back. It's not fair! Why are you doing this? Why are you helping me is it so you can hold it against me in the future?"

She stood up to say to Francis. He was confused and wondered what she meant by that. "Hold what against you? Your dad is sick and I am helping him because he has been my dad's best friend for a long time and the only reason they had a falling out was because of you and your boyfriend. I don't know how such a humble man could have had a daughter like you." He said and walked away. Bella tried to reach out to her after that but she screamed and ran further into the garden and found a quiet place to pour out her emotions.Everything had been done behind her back and it hurt her but she was not angry at Francis because she knew daddy had a part to play he would have convinced him to keep it a secret from her but Francis could not bear to do it. She decided to go and speak to daddy. To clear things up and let him know that she was aware.

When she went back into his room she saw daddy's eyes and it was sure of what she was going to say. They had the same eyes and it spoke to each other. It expressed complete emotions and it made her want to cry even more. She hugged him so tight and she asked him why he did not tell her about the pain he had been feeling or the doctor's scan he had gone through and he plainly said that he did not want to worry her and made Francis promise not to tell her but he did. She was right again. Her intuition was definitely really on point at times but not always.Daddy was her best friend even more than all the friends she had and she was going to lose him. She was going to lose yet another person in her life and after this she was going to be alone. All alone because her friends cannot be there for her all the time since they had their own lives as well. "Honey, after I'm gone, you are going to continue your studies and you are going to get a good job.

You are not obligated to work as someone's servant anymore. If you owe Francis anything you can use my savings to pay him back. Your daddy is going to be with your mama and I'm sad to leave you but I'm excited to date her up there." He joked and she started crying even more because she could not imagine completely losing him out of her sight.

"I will always love you and I forgive you so please forgive yourself and forgive me if I have hurt you in any way my baby piglet. Doctor says I have two months with you so we can chill." He joked and made her laugh a little. "Francis wanted you to have a good time at the event that's why he brought you there it's not just to hide this." He reassured her. "But it was part of the reason. I will always love you, daddy." She replied. He agreed with a nod. She held him close and could not bare to let go. These two months she was going to help him do whatever it is that he wanted to and she would get it done at any cost. That's what he would do if she were in his place. Their eyes lit up just being next to each other and it was a wonderful feeling and a beautiful bond.

# CHAPTER NINETEEN

———∞∞∞———

## *The start of a Goodbye*

*How will we ever say such a
strong word like goodbye?*

*N*athan William L, the epitome of a perfect daddy who gave his daughter love and sacrifice. He taught her forgiveness and strength. A good son, a good husband and a good father not everyone can be that but clearly Nathan showed his daughter that he could be a triple threat as such. Also a great friend that even though he and Stan Ray had a falling out he was still cared for by his best friend because he was such a loyal and genuine best friend to him for many years. A very honest and a person filled with gratitude. Stella wrote about her daddy in her diary. In fact she started a new one for *his journey towards the big good bye* and that's what she called it. Something not easy to do but she did it anyway. She also filmed videos of him everyday. His smile, his laugh and all their conversations were being filmed on her new phone that she bought specially for the sake of daddy. All these moments she was going to rush to capture and treasure all the days of her life. Cancer killed her mother and now it was going to take her father. It was a painful journey to see him go through chemo because it weakened him but he had so much resilience he fought the weakness.

She could not understand the journey of loss as a child but she could grasp it as a young adult holding on to every little piece of joyful moments that she could gather. Each joyful moment came with a piercing pain. It was not physical but it was emotional and draining. He screamed at times because it hurt and she felt that hurt not physically but she could just feel it. In the morning he would be fine and at night he would moan in pain. He lost more weight and hair but she constantly reminded him how handsome he was. Looking back at her parents young time photos, they were definitely a great looking couple. Everyday she made him tell her stories about his young life and how he met her mother. How they fell in love and what they felt when they found out they had her. Nathan loved getting Francis to sit in with them and Stan Ray. She was a little selfish with her time with him but daddy did not want that. Her friends came to visit as well whenever they could and also to be with her. She had two beautiful friends and they were her greatest gifts. Who helped to take care of daddy at a time when there was no one else.

After everyone left on a daily it made her happy to have time to chat with daddy on her own and Francis gave her that time.

Daddy reminded her of one friendship though that she did not treasure as a child. "There was this little boy who saw you as a gift. He was always so happy to come over to our place to spend time with you. You both enjoyed each other's company but I don't know what happened after that. Rocket influenced you to hate the world and only listen to him." Her daddy implied. She had absolutely no comeback this time around and just remained silent. This was not the time to argue with him especially when he was in the right and always will be. "Daddy, when we are kids we don't understand the measure of someone's presence or kindness in our lives. It's so far from our presented thoughts and the older get those thoughts just come back to bite and you and devours your emotions completely and you can't forgive yourself no matter how many times you try. Daddy it's hard for me to forgive me especially when I feel like karma keeps hitting me. You're being taken away from me for good." She stated. Her father held her held in his like he always does and teared. Her pain was always his pain and vice versa. They're each other's rock and very soon she was going to lose her rock for good.

Even though she technically did for a long time. Her ground was always rather shaky because it never gave her something solid to fall back on except the job she held or the nasty boss who seemed to be constantly saving her for reasons she could not understand. Did he hate her? But why would he still care? These were constant questions swimming in her head. Her persistence in spite of believing in his complete and utter hatred for her to do her job is probably the strongest reason why he would be so kind even though he came off as a jerk at times. After she finished her time with daddy and overthinking about her boss, she finally went out to work with Bella in the kitchen to prepare supper for Francis and his cousin. Stan Ray was away again and ever so often he stayed out of town. Stella Marie was still on a mission to reach out to Agnes but she needed to do it without overstepping her boundaries. It was not easy to do that because Francis was very sharp and he would probably call her out on anything she might do or say to his overprotected cousin that he was overprotective.

She was ready to serve supper when she overheard their conversation. They spoke rather loud so she could not be blamed, really. "He never stopped hitting me and the moment he forced me…I escaped and called the police." Agnes was saying and just at that moment she walked towards them to serve supper and Francis signalled to Agnes not to say anything. Agnes thanked Stella Marie and then held Stella's arm when she noticed there was a scar on her right arm as she was wearing a short sleeved shirt. "Who did this to you?" She asked her. Stella was hesitant to answer when she noticed Francis looking at her but it was the only way she could probably connect to Agnes and reach out to her. "My ex did this to me." Francis kept silent and did not stop her from speaking but she herself decided to stop there and get back to the kitchen. Agnes and Francis just looked at each other after that and continued to talking to each other. Stella went back to the kitchen and focused on her work but she was genuinely concerned for Agnes's wellbeing and wanted to make sure she was able to reach out to her since she was here. Maybe her scar could help her connect with her better.

Her natural instinct to care for someone else became stronger after all that she had been through with Rocket. Though it made her stronger, it had also made her more selfless pushing her to care for daddy the way that she did. She found her independence when she went through an ordeal as such. Her aim was to use her pain as a way to connect and heal others and in all this she seemed to have found her purpose. Daddy did tell her to go and find another career after it was his time to leave. Maybe her calling is within her current thought itself. Sometimes thoughts are an inspiration when it comes out of nowhere and gives you a purpose for your existence in a split second. When you are on the verge of losing something or already have lost something, you will eventually be on a journey to find yourself and your purpose. These things are gradual and she knew it. She knew it's not going to happen right away and that everything has it's time but when you catch a positive thought to do something worthwhile hold on to it until you can make it happen. Stella was determined that her purpose was getting clearer but first she had to face the reality of saying goodbye to her daddy, even that was gradual. Just as she was deep in thoughts Francis came by the kitchen and signalled at her to come out.

"When did that happen? The scar, was it recent?" He asked her. She was lost for words for a while before she could answer. "It's quite sometime actually, he's very strong and I couldn't fight him so he dragged me by the arm and then by the hair." Francis just listened until she had stopped talking.

"Agnes um.. would need a friend right now and I think you would be perfect. I can listen to her but I cannot connect and understand the way you would be able to. Please try to spend time with her ok?" He asked politely and she agreed. Bella watched as they spoke to each other from afar and smiled. When Stella turned around and went into the kitchen she noticed her smile.

"Why are you smiling?" She asked her. "Nothing sweetie, it's nice to see Francis asking you for help in a polite and not in a slave-driving way." Bella replied and Stella laughed. She suddenly did not feel so alone. Like there was something for her to do and someone else for her to care for other than daddy. That would be a void that she will never be able to fill when he leaves the world and mostly her world. *Goodbye*, it's tough but it's ever present. It's one of her most hated words to use and now she was going to hate it even more. Her mind was filled with inspiration and sad thoughts as much as her heart was filled with encouragement and heaviness. The heart and the mind gelled as much as the soul. They went together at times and they were apart at times because they were distant from each other. It was quite complicated and quite straightforward at times. There were things she understood and things she could not grasp. It was rather a battle constantly. Stella excused herself from work to write a letter to the word she hated. She started writing to inspire herself to release the anxiety and overcome her depression.

*Dear Goodbye,*

*You seem to love coming to me all the time. Taking away what was important to me in many ways. I dislike you or rather I hate you. You are an uninvited guest in my life but you keep creeping up on me, You keep dragging away what I hold most dear. This is new to me, writing to something I dislike but it helps me when I let you know how I do not want you around. STOP! Stop coming to me, don't stand in between daddy and me. It's not fair! You're not fair! Why? Why do you want to do this to me. Why? Why Mama and Daddy? I'm alone because of you or rather I am going to be alone. I hate you goodbye, I hate you so much.*

*Yours Truly,*
*Stella Marie*

She cried as she wrote the letter and thereafter placed it in an envelope and kept it in her cupboard. It was short and sweet but it helped her release or her mind would actually be a stock market. In life you either know nothing or you know something but you would never reach the point of knowing everything because everything takes a lifetime and not everyone has that much time. Daddy and Mama's timeline worried her about her own. What if she had lesser time that both of them together? What if she never even gets to accomplish all that she wanted to? It worried her. She had to do something more than be a helper to Francis. She had to accomplish something in her life and she had to do it fast because *goodbye* seemed to like her a lot. Determined to make daddy's last days comfortable and assuring she did all that she could to bring joy to him. Her daddy is the light that she needs and always will be in every way. He always inspires to fly even when she feels her wings have been tied up. Sooner or later she needs to release those wings and fly.

Daddy was so happy to see his daughter walk in and greet him with the beautiful smile that reminded him of his wife. "Hey mama's little photocopy. The older you get the more you resemble her. I miss that smile and I still get to see it and I'd like to believe I see the original copy real soon." When daddy said that she could not hold back the tears. That was a statement of him preparing for the *goodbye* that she dreaded. Daddy looked like that statement brought him joy instead.

He could not wait to be released from this bed and pain that he had to withstand and put on a brave face for his little piglet. He was gonna miss her but he believed that he would always be watching over her. "I'm contented sweetie, I did a great job, I married the love of my life and I help bring a beautiful gift, my daughter into this world. I lived and I lacked nothing, nothing at all. You were the greatest thing that I am glad to say I helped make happen." Daddy finished with a joke. Stella smiled still with tears in her eyes looking at her daddy with so much love she could not even describe. No one could ever possibly measure up to the man he has been in her life. That is what she believed.

Francis entered the room and startled her she quickly got up to leave but he signalled to her to sit back down. "The doctor is here to check on your dad you need to give them a little space." So they both left the room for the doctor to do as he needed. She felt like she hardly had much time to spend with him since she was told that she only had 2 months left with him. Every time she did get a little time there were always disruptions and it annoyed her a little. Francis felt a little bad for cutting her "visiting hours" with daddy short but there was really no choice. Procedures had to be carried out for his comfortable stay and they did all that they could. "I have two months with him and it's already the first week and I have to spend less than 10 mins with him and I am really frustrated. I'm sorry but I have to speak out because this job that I am doing is only for him and I am gonna leave once he leaves me. I'm just letting you know in advance." She said to him. Francis heard her out before he replied. "What about all the money you would probably owe me after this. Don't you want to work for it?" He asked her. "I can work somewhere else and pay you back, I promise I will." She reassured him. With that she walked away and got back to her duty post which was almost everywhere in the huge house. He had no words to say and just went back to check in on Nathan. The doctor was almost done so Francis decided to sit in with Nathan and have a chat since his daughter was upset and walked away.

Nathan greeted him when he saw him walk in and pull up the chair. "How are you son, Stan is a busier man than his movie star son, I see. Always on the go." Nathan joked.

Francis laughed at it and then responded "Yeah he does not want to slow down on the business he built. I was willing to support him but he says that I should focus on my future and he'll take care of his until he really needs me then he will let me know."

Nathan smiled knowingly to that response, that his best friend is a very strong willed and independent person. "That's why he had the strength to raise a son who does not carry his blood but carries his heart. Blood's not always everything it's the heart that connects people. Some people carry the same blood but they don't even have love for each other the way Stan Ray has loved you and your mum." Nathan called it. "All these years not being able to talk to him has been the worst years of my life. He's my brother through and through by heart, like I said. The heart connects more than blood." With that he teared. Francis reached out his hand and placed it on Nathan's in a reassuring manner. "Please forgive me. You have to so does your dad this is my goodbye forgiveness request. Please forgive my daughter as well she is my life and I'm leaving her behind and it pains me that she waited for me so long just to say goodbye for good. She hates goodbyes. Can you promise me something?" He asked Francis and he agreed.

"Please watch out for her it would really mean a lot to me." He held his hand tightly as he made his request. "Always. I will Mr N." He promised him. After that he left him to get some rest as the treatment had made Nathan tired.

Agnes on the other hand was restless and went to find Francis to have a chat but stumbled across Stella instead who was working with Bella who prompted her to go and see to Agnes. "Hi." Agnes greeted as soon as she saw her. "Hey, do you need something?" Agnes then replied that she was looking for Francis to talk but Stella offered to be her listening ear instead. Agnes poured out to her how the person she loved the most abused her and kept her quiet by threatening her not to tell anyone for 2 years straight and she was engaged to him. His abusive ways just got worst so she ran away and her cousin opened his doors to her in her worst time possible. She recalled how scared she was to wake up everyday and to face him because they had lived together.

A person who has been abused can adopt anxiety quite quickly and as for Agnes, going to sleep at night was a true torture. Stella experienced insomnia for a long time too and hers was every issue jumbled into one. She sat down and continued to listen to Agnes because sometimes all someone needs is a listening ear especially from someone who understands. She felt so calm and relieved to talk to Stella and vice versa. They really clicked well and an hour had passed since they talked. Francis had a little peek of them talking and it put a smile on his face to see his cousin smiling a little at least. He went into his home office to get things done for himself. He helped Stan Ray out with a little bit of the business when he was not out filming. It made him feel settled to help his father out in anyway he could. It's the least he felt he could do for someone who raised him as his own and gave him his surname after his own father messed his mother's life up and he was too young to grasp the intensity of the situation but he gradually listened to his mother and understood her. She definitely was blessed with Stan Ray both of them were and he constantly thanked God for him.

Everything in life can be a blessing even if it's bad it can be turned into a blessing because we should never despise the small and tough situations for these are the things that will make us stronger. It made him achieve his dreams and be restored which definitely built absolute gratefulness in him. He was a hardworking man as he was a hardworking little boy who fought all the negativity he received to become successful. He had a worry at the back of his mind and this worry was not just about his cousin but a certain someone. A certain staff of his who seemed to be his concern at this point. She worked so hard for her father only to lose him at the end and he was worried that she would go astray or go back to where she was hurt once she was left alone in this world. He carried a promise to her father and that was to keep an eye out for her so that was what he was going to do.

Stella and Agnes had finished talking and Agnes went back to rest while Stella had her duties to accomplish. Bella was heading home to spend time with her grandkids for the weekend so Stella was going to shoulder all her responsibilities as well.

They always helped each other out and mostly Bella always walked the mile for her so she worked hard and fast to help her out also she wanted to cramp in some time for daddy. As soon as she was done she went in to sit in the room with him though he had fallen asleep so she decided to sleep there for the night next to him. Nathan got up at night as he was in pain and saw his baby girl next to him. He took a bit of his blanket to cover even though he had no strength to do so. His body had weakened so much and he was getting frail quickly but his mind was ever so strong and determined to enjoy his last days. He could not do much but he could spend time with his baby girl in the littlest and most beautiful way.

Like just allowing her to feel his presence next to her while she was asleep like he always did when she was little. That was how he put her to sleep just by her knowing he was next to her and that made her fall asleep instantly and it felt nostalgic doing that again. He teared as he knew that as much as it hurt her to say goodbye to him, it was breaking him apart to say good bye to his little piglet. He leaned over despite of his pain to kiss the back of her head as she slept and whispered *daddy will always love you my ray of sunshine*.

The next morning she jumped up as she realised that there was no alarm next to her and she might be late but she was not. *Thank God*. When she woke up daddy was still asleep so she covered him up nicely with the portion of the blanket that she realised was on her. She slept really well without lying down compared to all the other days in her other room. With Francis's permission she was going to this everyday for 2 months if it was fine but it was going to cause a backache for sure but it did not matter because daddy was worth a backache.

He would have done the same for her indeed. Time was moving fast even though she wanted it to move slower and it was seriously breaking her apart. *Goodbye* was rearing its ugly head and she was not thrilled about it at all. Why did all her worst enemies always show up even the most invisible that was only just a word. A word had become her enemy and it was the worst ordeal for her at this point. Sometimes ignoring things really does not help it just makes it worst and piles up. The nurse was already in to attend to daddy.

Francis was already in the living room with Agnes waiting patiently for his cup of coffee and she rushed to get it for him. When she brought it to him he did not even look up as both of them were busy on their phones not even concern about their surroundings which made Stella to catch his attention by passing it over to him. He just stared at her and grabbed it from her hands.

She did not respond but just diverted her attention over to Agnes asking her if she needed anything and she politely declined. Francis was not in the best mood apparently because he had not shown her that much attitude in a while and he was clearly showing her some. She was confused but still just did as she needed to. When she came to him with some breakfast and informed him, he did not respond either. "Your breakfast is here." Agnes told him after she noticed that he ignored Stella.

"I don't want it. You can take it back Stella Ma..." He actually almost mentioned her full name but it was not in the best circumstance because he was upset about something and she did not know what. "Okay I will take it back." She replied and then went ahead to the kitchen. Her heart was feeling a certain sense of heaviness and she had no idea why other than the fact that she was going to lose daddy, she felt a slightly different sadness. *Was her boss not talking to her properly wearing her emotions down as well?*

# CHAPTER TWENTY

---·ᴑᴥᴑ·---

## *July 11ᵗʰ*

*We were not supposed to meet this soon*

*I*t had been 3 weeks since Francis A.K.A Roderick had spoken to her properly and a couple of days after their conversation he went away for filming a new project and that gave her more time with Agnes and Bella. They got to enjoy their ladies time once two out of three were done with work. Daddy was also very entertained by their company from time to time. July 10ᵗʰ was the day he would get back from his filming and she had to face his attitude again. She had no idea whenever his mood changes would occur. It was ever so often where he suddenly started being kind to her and then days where he started being mean to her. She still did not know what she had done this time. Well she knows he still holds past grudges at least that is what she thinks. It was July 9ᵗʰ and that was the day that they were on and the house had to look perfect for his return. Agnes was very helpful and did not want to sit around and do nothing so she helped them out and enjoyed doing that. Stella and *her girls* had the best of time. Hers and Bella's aim was to cheer Agnes up and give her the best time and they aced it for sure. They made her forget about all the abuse she had endured from her fiancé.

Stella left their side after a while to go spend sometime with daddy as she knew he was awake. The nurse saw her walk in so she gave them some privacy. He was weaker but he still found the strength to talk to her and smile. "I love to see your mama's smile, I'm on medication…i'm a little..high." He struggled to say. It had already been a month and they were only given two to be by each other's side. Stella smiled knowing her daddy was trying to crack a joke.

It had been 3 weeks of seeing him get weakened and it was hard but she probably had 3 more weeks with him and making him comfortable was her priority. She really worked hard on that and everything she did for him she did it with class. Gave him all his favourite foods, favourite shows, clothes. All the things he loved was presented to him.

Including her time and conversations and going through old albums with him so he could admire the beauty of his wife because ever since he weakened he kept mentioning that he could see her and that she came to visit him every single time. Stella would listen and then go to one side and cry. When someone speaks this way it could mean that they are ready to go to the other side. She was very disturbed and yet she had to listen to him and shown him her full attention. Whatever he struggled to speak. "I..love you.. my little piglet." He spoke up and he did that every single day she went to sit with him. "I love you daddy, I always will. You are my light and I hope you keep shining your light on me ok?" She said as she cried. "Your mama..and me we will al..ways shine a light in and for you baby..g.irl." He spoke in pauses struggling to catch his breath. Stella Marie cried and rested her forehead on his hand. Nathan teared too as he could not hold back at all. They both were going through the emotions leading up to the goodbye and he wanted to be honest with her because he truly felt the pain of having to leave her behind. Sometimes people who are dying are not able to spend time with the ones they love or tell them how they feel and when their demise is sudden it leaves a lot of regrets of unsaid words, unrequited feelings and he did not want his baby girl to be left in such a state and she wanted to give him the best last days anyone could ask for.

"Daddy, I wrote you a letter and I want to read it to you." She said to him and he agreed to it.

*Dear daddy,*

*I am the most blessed girl to have an amazing daddy like you, not many girls can say this. You showed me grace when I certainly did not deserve it. You picked me up when I was left on the ground and though I chose to hurt you, you did not show me your broken heart but you helped heal mine in all the stages of my life you have been through with me. You raised with the love of a mother and protection of a father. Again, not many girls get to say that. I do. I always will. If I ever have a daughter I am going to tell her that I am strong because I received the best love from the best man in my life and the best parents ever.*

*I received a beautiful love of a father. If I have a son I am going to tell him all about you and the kind of man he should learn to be is who you are, daddy. You are the best example of a man with character and that character is of a person that I would want my daughter to marry and my son to be. If I never have children of my own I will adopt some and still tell them about you. My world has been a great place even with all the pain because I always had my angel and always will have my angel holding my hand and guiding me just like you did unashamed.*

*I will never be able to find another person like you in my life and even if I do they would never measure up. My light, my love, my inspiration is you, daddy. My everything.*

*Love,*
*Stella Marie(Your baby piglet)*

She could see tears flooding his eyes as they were in hers. These are the words that she needed to tell him before she never got to see his reaction and that is the best thing to do to see someone's reaction when you speak to them from your heart and not hold back until it is too late. She even recorded this moment as she read his letter and saw his reaction as she had been doing everyday. It was too precious. Every moment was precious and from now on she was going to take each moment seriously. "Thank you...You will be blessed." He replied and kissed her on the forehead as he always did.

Meanwhile, Agnes and Bella were outside busy cleaning up as they wanted to give Stella some time more. "M'dear Bella, Francis has not brought a girl home for a long time has he?" Bella laughed when she heard Agnes ask that. "He has a hard time holding on to any relationship or casual dating because there is something he needs to let go of or fix rather." Agnes did not understand what Bella meant or maybe she did but she just kept silent and continued on with what she was doing. It definitely had to do with someone in the house. Stella Marie had walked out of the room wiping tears from her eyes. Agnes and Bella knew about the letter she wrote and hugged her as soon as they saw her. "Are your hands dirty?" She asked them a short while later and the two nodded which led them all to burst out laughing.

Every moment even these little moments with her girls were *GOLD* that it inspired her to collect every moment like it was a firefly that could easily fly away so you had to catch it and keep it closed so it would not get away where you could store it like it was your treasure in a jar. Life is rapidly changing every second and Stella already was faced with many big changes and she had not accomplished a career or lived out her dreams yet because everything had been put on hold. So whatever she could get that was good for her she learnt to appreciate because no good thing comes easy and endurance will build one's character towards success and shape your attitude to be better towards even the most negative aspect of life.

Her next hurdle will be learning how to cope with daddy's demise for now she could see that she was not going to be alone but what will really happen when that moment comes. When she has to go through burying him and not be able to hold his hand or see his smile anymore. The thoughts creeped up on her every once in a while even when she was focused on carrying out her job.

Bella noticed her in deep thoughts as she was cleaning. "How clean do you want the floor to be sweetie?" She asked her jokingly. Stella stopped and just knelt to the ground and started sobbing. Bella knelt down in front of her and hugged her. "You are not alone, I am here with you. So is Francis along with Stan Ray. We are going to be with you through this journey." Bella showed her what she needed warmth, love and reassurance. "You're my baby girl and I feel you, everything that you are going through when I hug you I can feel it, so I got you,I got you." She said to her and they both were in tears.

After the day was done she laid her head down on her pillow, looked up at the ceiling and she prayed. *Dear God, if there is one I could ask from you, please take care of daddy, like he took care of me or even better. Since you want him back so fast you need to love him and care for him. He needs to be reunited with mama, if they can remember each other. Make sure they always watch over me.Thanks.* With that she slept.

The next morning everyone hurried and scurried like little mouses preparing for the bosses return. Stella was in to check on dad for a quick bit before she rushed over to help Bella out while Agnes slept in because she did not want Francis to know that she had been helping them out while he was away or he would be furious. She was very precious to him a sister he really would go all out for so he would want to see her do the work he had paid people to do. He had arrived on time at 9am like he said he would. His first stop once he reached home was to check in on Nathan so that gave the rest of them time to be ready for him and his requests. Nathan was so happy to see him after 3 weeks and Francis noticed that he was weaker than he had been. He quickly called up his doctor to come by because he was worried and sat by his side.

Nathan was trying to talk the whole time but his words were slurred and he was struggling so he asked the nurse who informed him that she had just given him some *Morphine* to ease the pain he had earlier.

He did not want to let Stella know anything because clearly it would mess her up and it's not something she needed. So he quietly stayed by Nathan's side and waited for the doctor. Since he was struggling to talk he tried to get him to type but his hands were even weaker. It took some time but the doctor arrived and quickly rushed to check on him and his body had really gone through so much in a course of a day because the cancer cells were spreading everywhere and his body was too weak to fight it. He was groaning in constant pain and he was restless. The doctor advised Francis to let Stella know what was going on because Nathan might not pull through much longer. So he agreed to go and speak to her right away.

Francis went to look for her and found her in the guest room cleaning up. He cleared his throat three times before he got her attention and when he finally did she looked scared like she always did whenever he came around. Or the perfect word would be *intimidated* which was what it truly was she was truly intimidated by him throughout this whole journey and even more so when she found out who he was. He was nervous this time to talk to her because he this was even heavier news than the last one.

"Your dad.." He only said that and tears filled her eyes. "Um…he's not dead but he's weak and the doctor said the cancer has spread so you need to spend time with him because…" He could not finish his sentence because she left the room before he could say anything more she just dashed past him.

She ran to daddy's side while crying so hard she could not breathe and knelt down beside his bed but she could not even touch him because he was so weak. He was struggling to speak but he managed to drag his words out and said *I love you*. She replied "I love you daddy, I love you so much. I'll stay by your side so that you'll get better okay." She did not leave the room at all she stayed close to him the whole night and the next morning,she slept in. When she woke up she felt so heavy emotionally and could not feel her arms because she slept on it for a long time. She looked up at daddy and his eyes were closed. He was still asleep and she did not want to disturb him, so she took the blanket to cover him but as her hand touched his it felt cold. She tried waking him up but he did not respond and she checked his pulse and she could not feel anything so she screamed for help and nurse came rushing in with Bella and Francis.

After doing a check they called in the doctor and an ambulance came with him and Nathan was pronounced dead for quite some time. It was already 9am, July 11th. Bella held Stella Marie so tight as she screamed and cried while Francis covered Nathan's body with the blanket. He was in tears as well and texted his father to let him know the news. Stan Ray was already on his way over. The people from the morgue came over to get his body and Francis was already getting funeral preparations done with help from his friend over the phone.

Stella suddenly could not feel at all, her whole frame felt numb and she passed out in Bella's arms. Thank God the medical team was still around to help out and attended to her. Agnes had just come in from her morning jog and realised she had missed a lot after checking in with Francis and both of them rushed to Stella's room where the nurse and Bella were taking care of her as she was on drips after passing out and an oxygen mask.

She was conscious after a while but she was resting. They were by her side and Francis asked Agnes to stay on while he went to receive his father at the door who was in tears and Francis hugged him so tight to comfort him. He had lost his best friend after just reconciling with him. It was painful to know that time was not in our hands and that we need to hold everyone precious to us closer than we hold things because we can get things back but we cannot get our precious ones back once they leave us.

"Nathan was supposed to wait for me, he did it again he left me again." Stan Ray said and he sat down. He was broken by yet another loss in his life. Losing his wife was painful and losing his best friend was dreadful that he could not hold back and as a grown man he cried yet again. He quickly drifted to his concern for Stella and what she must be facing at this point, all the brokenness she must be holding on to. Stan Ray is a great father to his son and his father's heart was concerned for this girl who has just been completely orphaned after sacrificing all her years fighting to save her father's life. When Stan Ray walked into the room Stella had just opened her eyes and she was feeling really weak and tears were still falling from her eyes. He went over to her and sat by her bedside whilst Agnes got up and gave way to her uncle. He sat down and when she saw him she started crying even more. "Stella, listen we are here for you, you are not alone young lady. You are your daddy's pride and joy, my best friend's pride and joy and I am going to be here for you okay?"

He placed his hand on hers and she was broken beyond repair at this point that she could not even talk. Francis came in and stood by his dad's side placing his hands on his left shoulder. Grieve was in his home today and everyone was mourning loss of a really good man who lived a beautiful life helping others and being kind to almost everyone he met. His funeral was not going to be empty for sure. Nathan was sacrificial and everything he did was for someone else's happiness and Stan Ray could testify to this. The amount of help that Nathan gave him was the most that anyone has ever done for him. He had gratefulness and he could only render that right now through Stella. She was and always will be the importance of Nathan William L's life. They all went to rest as the funeral was just the next day.

The next morning, Stella was back on her feet and she felt empty as she stood in front of the room where daddy slept. It was as empty as her heart and she couldn't feel anything at that moment but emptiness. Like her life had just left the phase of the earth. He had been her life all these years, by her working hard to keep him alive and just like that his life was cut short after he was given a second chance to live. *It's not fair.* She thought out loud in frustration and when she turned around she saw Bella standing behind her, listening. "Honey, life is not fair but life is an opportunity. An opportunity for you to pick yourself up and finally live your life for you, that's what he wanted for you. You remember?" When Bella asked Stella agreed that she did indeed remember her father telling her to get an education and a better career. Bella then told her to report to Francis's office where he was waiting to speak with her.

When she reached there she noticed there was an envelope in his hand and she diverted he gaze back to his eyes that were staring unsparingly at her. End Her first thought was that she was going to be fired and he wrote her letter to officiate her firing but shortly after her thoughts were interrupted by him wanting to speak to her. "This letter is for you, your father wanted you to read it after he took his leave but you can only read it after the funeral today." He noted to her and she reached out her hand to take the envelope from his but he held on to it and did not let go. At that moment she realised she had been a little too close for comfort so she stepped back after letting go of the letter. "Actually, I'm sorry I wasted your time, I am going to hold on to this." With that she left the office and went straight down to dress up and get into the car to leave to the church.

She was still confused but she was not in the right state of mind to question her boss just yet. Bella rode together with Stella and Ren while Francis & Agnes went with Stan Ray in his car.

Bella as usual the moral support that Stella appreciates very much so. Once they reached the church it was packed with people she had never met. Stan Ray apparently knew some people because they were mutual friends through Nathan. As the priest came forward to open the service and do the prayers.

Stella was invited forward to prepare for a Eulogy. Which she definitely not prepared for. She bought a lot of time when the priest decided to extend the message. The moment had finally come when she had to go up to speak. She looked down at the coffin with her father's peaceful face. He was smiling like he always loved to. "Daddy…" She stopped to hold her tears and catch her breath. "First of all, he was the best daddy a girl could ask for, he had an energy of sunshine. Brightened every dull moment I had ever had to go through. He had to do motherly things as well and it was hilarious. He had no idea what kind of sanitary pad to get me but he learnt and got me what I needed. He always had a friend over and a friend wherever he went. Everybody knew his name Nathan William L. He was remarkable and charming any woman would fall at his feet but his eye was for mama, only for mama.

He loved her like she was a diamond that he would treasure with his life. He made her happy as much as he possibly could. When they fought he would sing one of mama's favourite songs. *Yesterday Once More* by the carpenters. *When I was young I would listen to the radio.* She tried to sing but she could not continue because she started crying. Bella went up to offer her a tissue. "Daddy was strong-willed and he taught me to be that girl but I was too dependent on him and it only worked when he was not responsive during his stroke. He fought to come back for me, although it was my fault he became that way in the first place." She paused to cry and then wiped her tears. "I lost the best I ever had and I don't know where to go from here but I'll figure it out for him.

He carried the role of a mother and father without remarrying he had a tough job on his hands, me. Yet he did it with poise and patience. No complaint at all and no disappointment even when I disappointed him. Daddy you are the best that this lifetime has given me. I love you, rest in power." With that she ended and went forward to look at him in his coffin and gave him a flying kiss before she returned to her seat. Stan Ray took the pulpit next and he was tears.

"Hey bestie, you were the best friend a boy could ever need and a man could ever understand. Always finding ways to help someone and fighting for those you love no matter what the situation was.

You know we were friends since middle school and as we grew older and wanted to have girlfriends so badly, well he did, he only wanted one girl,when he met this beautiful girl, Rosemary. He chased her until she gave him attention. He did all he could in his power to make her his. She was so reserved and he was so confident that he could bring out of her shell. So he did they fell for each other eventually and when he was getting married, I was his best man. He was so nervous to see her walk out in that wedding dress, he turned to me and he said. I think I am going to see my angel....*he cried*..I am going to see my angel who will take me to heaven with her one day.

He cried as he saw her come out with her daddy in that beautiful white dress and he was crying. That was how in love he was and it was the first happiest day of his life. Then came the second, when Rosemary got pregnant and he found out he was having a baby girl. For nine months he waited and waited impatiently but he took care of a rosemary like a queen. We did up the baby's room and then when she finally came it was like he fell in love all over again. There was a sparkle in his eyes when he carried you and looked at you Stella Marie." He looked directly at Stella who was sitting there and she was lying on Bella's shoulder crying because she could not hold herself together. "Today I am going to call Francis up to read the letter he wrote to you a month ago. Francis."

With that Francis came up with the envelope in his hand and Stan Ray went to sit down. He cleared his throat before he spoke and he opened up the letter but before he read it, he had somethings to say. "Uncle Nate, was part of the joy of my childhood and he gave me so much to remember that were good memories.

Thank you for being a great friend to my family and I. This letter I am going to read, he gave me just for today. He wanted to be heard not just by his daughter but by everyone he cared for who may be in this hall." With that he opened the envelope and opened up the folded letter and prepared to read it.

*Dear Friends and Family,*

*Thank you for coming, though I can't quite catch up with ya'll right now, I just want to say, you completed my life each journey was absolutely stunning with you by my side. Stan Ray a big shoutout to you, bruh, like the young ones like to say.*

Stan Ray and the attendees laughed at that. Francis continued reading.

*I wanted to finally get out of that stroke so I could live it up again and spend time with you all. Whoever I have spent time with for those I haven't I appreciate your attendance. I never planned my life out, I lived in the moment and I appreciated every single moment I was alive and it never backfired on me. I want to encourage you not to be afraid to do what you need to do so that when you do it, you won't reach your grave regretting but you'll be like me happy that I have lived even though I was not given that much more time or I spent years not being able to do much but I have no regrets. I had the best parents, siblings. I had the best friend and amazing people around. I married the love of my life, my queen and she gave me a princess who I want to talk to now. Stella Marie, wipe those tears, you are strong. Everything was taken from you but you fought back for you and for me. You did not sit and cry over spilled milk or revenge the abusers. You moved on and you kept a pure heart. Forgiveness is not only for someone else it is also for you, daddy has forgiven his little piglet she needs to release that forgiveness to herself.*

Francis paused and looked up at her as he remembered saying almost the same thing to her.

*Daddy was given borrowed time to come back and write this letter to you but I could not speak to you so I wrote it all down. You are my second angel, my diamond that I would say God loved me so much to give to me. You are beautiful when you smile and when you cry. You are cute when you get mad it's fun to watch especially when you were little. You are not left alone. God brought us to a palace where my best friend and his son had a royal heart to take us into.*

*Bella a beautiful mama figure to you but you need to make something of yourself. I love you baby piglet I will not say the word you hate but I will say. I will always watch over you along with my beautiful girlfriend. Rosemary.*

*Shine bright*

*Daddy A.K.A Nathan William L.*

With that Francis left the pulpit and a few other people came up to speak before the priest closed the service with a prayer and a hymn *Amazing Grace*. Everyone came forward to throw flowers in his coffin and Stella could not leave his side because the next part was the hardest.

The burial was the last time she could see him. The hearse came by and Francis, Stan Ray and a couple of her uncles who she did not even know came to help to carry the coffin. Bella and Agnes stayed by her side and so did her friends Marilyn and Jamie. She truly was not alone but she felt so alone indeed. She lost a part of her that she could never get back yet again.

When they reached the graveyard it was a painful process that many years ago she almost fell six feet under because she could not say goodbye. She buried her mother, she saw her child die in front of her and now she was going to bury her daddy. Her life has just seen death constantly and it was so frustrating. She was angry at God but daddy did not want her to be, he always asked her to keep the faith but at this moment she just could not. As the last rites were done it was time for her coffin to be lowered into the ground. Another six feet under that she had become used to. When the time had come for the coffin to be lowered. She felt her heart beating really fast it literally felt like it was going to pop out of her chest. She lost her balance and yet again as she cried almost fell in but this time she was caught by Francis who pulled her back and for the first time he hugged her and did not let her go as she cried.

She was not even aware who was holding her because she was too distraught. She then pulled apart from the hug and told everyone she would like to have few moments alone. Francis asked everyone to go ahead and waited for her. Stan Ray also left with the rest to go to their house for a lunch session. Stella sat by the lot where he father was buried. She held a rose in her hand and refused to put it on top and just wanted to talk to him. "Daddy. I need you to always watch over me okay? Now that you're busy with mama you both better make time for me..Or I'll not speak to you again." She said as she cried onto the rose, kissed it and then released it on top before getting up and leaving.

When she turned around she saw that everyone was gone except Francis in his car but she also felt like someone else was there watching her so she quickly rushed over to his car and got in. There was complete silence for the first ten minutes of the drive home. "You're gonna be okay, Stella Marie." He said as he concentrated on driving. She turned to look at him and then back in front. "Were you the one who pulled me back?" She asked and he just nodded in reply. "Thank you. This is the second time I almost fell in, the first time I was a kid." She said to him.

"Well, one day you're gonna have to be in there yourself so stop trying so hard when it's not your time." He replied and it made her laugh a little and he smiled and quickly wiped the smile off of his face. When they finally reached back, the guests was socialising and eating. Marilyn and Jamie ran over to hug her tight. "Stop trying to be buried okay? We need you here." Jamie reassured her while Marilyn laughed. Francis went over to spend time with his dad as he felt a little bit awkward among his friends.

"So hot boss saved you, that was cute." Marilyn pointed out and Stella just rolled her eyes while smiling. "It would have been cuter if I had not almost fallen in yet again." She replied. Her friends laughed. Bella was busy serving everyone with the kitchen helpers so Stella decided to go and help them. Whenever there were big events Francis always hired extra help because he really took care of and understood his staff very well. He refused to allow Stella to lift a finger and asked Bella to chase her out from the kitchen and she literally did that.

Stella was to only attend to her guests each and everyone of them and also to get to know her relatives who she really had no clue who they were. It was quite a strain having to keep a straight face and talk to everyone so she went to her room to take a timeout. Agnes noticed her going there and went to go check in on her.

"Stella, it's me Agnes can I come in?" She knocked on the door and Stella let her in. "Do you need anything?" Agnes offered and Stella declined. The next thing Agnes knew Stella had broke down and Agnes lent her a shoulder to cry on. "I can't talk to all this people it's exhausting. I want to go take a walk outside is that ok, if I go on my own?" Stella quickly changed her mind and Agnes agreed to let her go. When she went out she kept walking all the way out of the house compound and just kept walking straight. Her mind was blank and her heart was so heavy that led to tears pouring out of her eyes and she could not stop it that made her energy wear out really fast. As she was walking she had the same feeling she had at the grave yard that someone was watching her. It was a scary feeling indeed. She kept walking to ignore the feeling and she was pretty sure it was not a supernatural kind of feel it was a feeling of someone actually following her while watching her closely.

"Stella Marie, I am sorry for your loss. Truly sorry." The voice sounded very familiar and when she turned behind it was indeed Rocket. He never gave up no matter how many times he was warned. "I don't need your condolence you can keep it. What do you want?" She asked him. "Relax, I came to say goodbye. I am getting married to someone, she's pregnant and I want to move on I came to say goodbye. I wanted you to have something, this is your necklace that your dad bought for you on your sixteenth birthday. He gave it to me to keep it and I kind of stole it to sell it. Yesterday I found while clearing up the room and it had both yours and his picture. Didn't sell it either because I misplaced it.

Look I cannot change what I did, but I pray that you will forgive me for everything I did up until recently I don't know what I was thinking." She kept quiet for a while before responding and took the necklace from his hands "The only person who needs to forgive you is yourself.I hope to never see you again. Goodbye Rocket."

With that she turned around to leave and so did he. They officially parted ways and that helped her to show him her strength and that she was not afraid anymore. He definitely felt that as he thought about it. What she said to him struck him deep and it made him think as he walked away and brought him to tears but he quickly wiped it off. Loving someone and hurting them is really toxic. Wanting them but treating them like they were just a toy and that is what he did to Stella.

When she reached home after her short walk everyone were looking at her as if she committed a crime. Francis did not say anything and gestured to her to go ahead into her room. She sat in her room and started crying so much after controlling it all the way. She had to release her sadness and her frustrations that were both combined together. The poor girl was burdened and shattered. It all hit her at once being so heavy at that moment. She stayed in the room for a long time and the guests left. She refused to come out from the room to say goodbye to everyone.

Marilyn and Jamie stayed on and talked to Agnes and Stan Ray while waiting for her. Francis and Bella checked on her because it had been quite some time. Bella opened the door with the key she had and saw her sitting in a corner of the room looking messy and her eyes looked so heavy after all that excessive crying. Bella held her close without speaking she needed a warm touch not a questionnaire of what happened.

It was quite clear already that she was going through the aftermath of her loss. "Honey, we are here for you, always." Bella's concern made her feel relaxed and comforted. It was going to be a new journey for her as she had to take the step to do something other than working as a housekeeper.

# CHAPTER TWENTY ONE

———— ◦/◦/◦ ————

## *Restoration*

*We always seek to be restored*

Stella focused all her energy on work so that she would have to face her emptiness. The girl never had a chance to take a break from life it just seemed to keep moving in the unstable direction since she was a child. Years and years eaten up by the "*locusts*". Daddy's demise is just another add on reminder that she was never going to find happiness and those were thoughts that played in her mind when she was alone and doing nothing so that is why she kept busy. She did not want to sit and wallow in self pity. She wanted to have freedom and rest in her mind and soul so she had to keep her physical self moving and occupied. What else can you do when you keep losing every part of you and it never seems to stop? It makes a person wonder why they were even born was it just so they could go through life bleeding mentally and spiritually. So that they could get everything stolen while others who messed other people's lives up get it better? Questions that you never will find your own personal answer to.

She was battling in her mind it was so noisy in there that no music or distraction could quieten it down. It was so unfair to have to deal with it especially on her own. As she battled her thoughts and worked through it she felt a sudden rush in her heartbeat. It was a panic attack creeping up on her again and she quickly went to get some water and took deep breaths in and out. She was dizzy and felt really faint that not even the water could make her feel any better. Her heart was heavy and so was her head while her face looked really pale. She did not pay attention to anyone around her because she was so filled with weakness and despair like she was falling into a dark spiralling hole and she could not get out. It felt rather distressing. Chills filled her as her heart gave her unrest and she was on the verge of passing out no matter how much she tried to relax. Eventually, she passed out yet again and Agnes found her and quickly got some help to get her to checked on.

As she had not responded Agnes called the ambulance to come and take her to the hospital. Bella was out getting groceries at that time. When they reached the hospital, the put Stella on drips and gave her rest. Agnes stayed by her side to make sure she was okay but had to call and inform Bella and Francis on what had happened. Francis told her that he would make his way down to the hospital. It was only an hour later that Stella had woken up and looked around to find Agnes sitting by her side. "Hey, you're awake, I was worried sick." Agnes said to her. Stella smiled at her and felt amazingly well-rested with her presence well until her cousin arrived and Francis arrived it made her panic attack seem to arise. Agnes made it worst by leaving them alone to go to the restroom. "Why do you love passing out so much?" Was his first question to her. She did not know how to respond to that and then she did. "Passing out is not a hobby, sir. I just..I have panic attacks at times and it kind of sucks. It shuts me down and I can't do what I have to." She lamented him which made him regret passing that comment. He just kept silent and listened to her continue to rant on panic attacks and she refused to stop because she secretly wanted to annoy him until she could get him to leave but he did not. "I know what you are trying to do, you are trying to make me leave and I am not going to do that. I'm not going to let you win, Stella Marie." He said to her and that made her go completely silent and confused. *What did he mean by that?* She thought to herself. "I don't leave like I used to, I don't give up like I used to.

When you two did what you did along with your dimwit friends I stood up and fought back against the stereotypes my head told me I was. If you keep giving in to that, you are just a loser. Stop giving up and letting your thoughts win you don't have to stay this way." He continued.

He was actually encouraging her and she felt that even though she was really confused. She was discharged from the hospital on the same day and Francis brought the girls home. She was absolutely quiet during the ride home when Francis and Agnes were talking. They were trying to get her attention but she was in a daze and did not respond to them.

Stella went straight to her room when they reached home and rested with a little help from Bella who helped her out from the moment she arrived. Bella decided to leave her to have her own space and get some rest. She was tossing and turning on her bed and was not able to get any rest at all. It really worried her that she would fall deeper into anxiety and God forbid, depression. She wanted to do more with her life but how was she going to do it if she this attacks keeps going on.

It was a lot to take in after the loss of daddy and it felt absolutely heavy on her shoulders and she was not able to handle the burden she felt. She had people around her helping her but somehow she felt so alone and swamped with stress. Stella's life just kept teaching her more and more hard lessons and for her it really felt like extreme karma what had happened with daddy. Getting him back only to lose him for good it really hit her so hard. She did remember daddy telling her to get her life on track and moving on from this job to get a better career and future for herself but it did not seem that easy.

Change is never an easy thing when you have been so used to a certain kind of lifestyle for the longest time. Seeking out a new direction could be a really scary path to take when you have no idea where you want to head. For Stella she had been so used to just being a housekeeper and a caretaker to daddy that she did not have any motivation to pursue anything for herself.

Taking care of someone else and someone else's property had become apart of her and she was immune to it that she forgot what she liked or wanted which was terrifying to find out now. No it was not too late, but it was rather delayed. She was already a young adult and had lost her youth to responsibility caused solely by her irresponsible actions. She had no idea what her path was meant to be in the corporate sector as she had not been able to figure that out in the past years.

A lot was on her mind but nothing she was planning on doing with those thoughts. She chose to remain where she was for a specific time frame until she could figure her life out. That took a lot out of her and rest was far from her mind due to the overworking of it. The poor girl did not seem to catch a break at all.

*I will to be someone who never gives up on me.* Are words she whispered under her breath as she laid down and tried to get some sleep. She felt pathetic one moment and energised the next. Her battle was always within her and it never seemed to take a breather. She was scarred and she was battling hoping that she had no reason to bombard anyone else with her burdens. It was more than enough that Bella, Francis, Stand Ray and even Agnes had to take for her, even Ren the driver. She felt very obsolete if she had to make them always fight for her and not stand up for herself and seek independence. That was definitely a major setback for her that she was not able to find her purpose outside of having to take care of daddy. What could she possibly study or work as when she was a seasoned caretaker of a celebrity with a high status. One who cares for her and that still baffles her that he cares but he also threatens her so she was not really sure what his purpose in her life was as of this point.

*Girl, sleep.* She thought to herself. She needed to sleep and not just physically but mentally. As exhausted as her body was, her mind could not give her a break. The poor young woman gave her thoughts a lot of her attention and made it her priority that she forgot how it affects her anxiety levels when she overthinks.

It was spiking high because she could feel her heartbeat race to the highest level and she could hardly breathe. So she took a deep breath in and cleared her mind bit by bit that was when she felt better and more relaxed. She finally fell into a proper and deep sleep.

Her dreams messed with her a little and woke her up but only for ten minutes and she fell into deep slumber again. The next morning she was really relaxed and refreshed. She clearly had a really good sleep and was ever so ready to report to her duty post. As usual she prepared his breakfast and especially how he liked his coffee, strong. She went to give it him on his literal silver platter.

He asked her to sit down which she did not particularly want to but she did anyways but she noticed that he had an envelope for her. He handed it over to her and asked her to open it right away. When she did she saw an application form to a private college and a cheque written to her name. "You are going to apply to this college and the course list are online. It's part time so you can still work and study. Once you complete this you can move on with your life. You can work anywhere else, you don't have to work with me." He spoke confidently and that is one of the things she had liked to learn from him and that was his confidence.

From a kid who could not fight back for to save his life to the confident boss and successful person that he was. Life is a choice and building it up is a choice and Francis a.k.a Roderick was a great example of that. He made her promise that she would fill and submit the application right away as the finances were already in her hands. "You've got this. Your daddy believes in you. That cheque was from him and not me. He saved up all that money for you to study and he would have liked to give it to you himself but um..he passed it over to me. You are blessed Stella Marie, you have everything you need. Right where you are." He pointed out to her and she agreed with a nod and a grateful heart to daddy as well as Francis. She was going to work hard and achieve what she needed for herself and to make daddy proud. After she passed over the completed and sealed application to Ren to be mailed out she went back to work with a heart filled with encouragement. Gratefulness was definitely above that and she could not have asked for more. To see how blessed you are you really need to step back and look at all you have gained instead of complaining about all you have lost. Focus on what is in front instead of what is behind.

Stella Marie surely needed to work on that because she was very focused on her pain which keeps leading her down to the path of anxiety and it was really too much to take because it shuts her down completely at times. Bella saw her dash in to the kitchen with a big smile on her face and was naturally led to smile back because Stella really has a smile that lights up a room but rarely does use it. "You know I am so glad to see that smile, it is so rare but so beautiful Stella Marie." Bella had to say and Stella was very smitten by that compliment.

One thing she knew was if she made the decision to leave this job and take another part time job it would mean that she would have to leave behind a family she had gotten over here yes even Francis.

It was not something she wanted to do and she made her decision on the spot to work and live there while she did her studies so she ran back to the office to inform Francis of her quick decision. "What a quick decision that was." He responded after she had told him. "I want to be grateful and not just forget what has been helping me so long just because I get other opportunities. Of course after I complete my studies I will definitely look for another opportunity." When she said that Francis nodded in agreement.

Then he suddenly took a few steps forward and he happened to be really close to her then he looked at her directly in her eyes, placed both his hands on her shoulders and said, "We…believe in you all of us here and whatever you do you are not alone, Stella Marie. My dad, Bella, Agnes even Ren whichever way we can we will help you and I'm sure you have your friends too. Never ever feel alone." When he said that she had no words to say but tears streamed down her eyes and he hugged her. It was something she really needed and it felt like how daddy always made her feel, true comfort. When they pulled apart from the hug she whispered *Thank you*. Then he turned and walked back towards his table and she turned to leave the office. When he sat down at his desk he looked out the window thinking about what just happened he was guarding himself for so long in showing that much care but he promised Nathan that he would take care of his daughter and he was not a man who would go back on his word. Taking care of someone meant going all out at times even with your emotions you can't guard it too much when you are showing concern to someone. It was hard for him but he pushed through the difficulty.

Francis called his dad to talk to him over the phone, Stan Ray always knew the right words to say to his son when he was in a state of confusion or unrest. In fact anything Francis went through, his whole life he could depend on his father to uplift him and make him feel better. "Son, you are a good man and whatever you do won't be done in vain. I know my son, he's a man of his word." Stan Ray reassured him over the phone.

That put a smile on Francis's face and he was very inspired to be better. Every time he had time spent with his dad there was lot of encouragement in his heart that he hardly could get anywhere else not even from his manager who pushed him to the limits at time and never gave him a break. Sometimes he felt like giving up on his acting career and just focus on carrying on his father's business since he has already helped him so much in it. He was privileged and he appreciated it by using his privilege to help others.

Stella was out in the garden taking a breather and thinking through things. All these things happened to her real quick and it was quite overwhelming. She did not know how she was going juggle school and work at the same time but she had to build that confidence in herself along the way and it was not going to be a walk in the park, that she knew.

She loved writing and it helped her to relax. So the garden was her new place to write and relax when all the work there was done then she had time for herself. She wrote letters to herself and that's when she had placed her whole heart into words that gave her release she had not felt when she bottled everything up inside, obviously. Tears streamed down from her as she released all her emotions onto a page of her diary. She recollected all the things she lost and how it felt like little by little everything was being restored to her. It felt beautiful and energising to write. The course that she was going to take was also related to writing. She had to sit for an entrance test in order to begin the course. She wrote all she was anticipating in her diary and it made her feel absolutely ready but what worried her at the back of her mind was the actual journey. In her mind it all felt good but when everything played out in reality it would not be as simple. She knew that for sure but she had to prepare herself for it. As she wrote her thoughts there was someone appearing on her mind and it was out of nowhere because her thoughts were not related to him. Francis and the hug they had where she was vulnerable with him for that short time kept playing in her mind. He talked to her, he looked her in the eye and assured her that he *saw* her.

A moment of flashback to that moment kept her from writing but she snapped back to reality and then she wrote the whole moment down so that she would never forget it not that she will because it was on her mind.

Just then as she was busy writing she was startled by a presence standing by the garden chair. It was *him* the guy she was busy scribbling about. She quickly closed her diary the moment he asked if he could sit next to her and she agreed. *What's he doing here, it is my break!* She spoke in her mind.

"Don't worry I'm not pushing you back to work I just need air too and we have only have one chair." He joked. "I did not say anything." She replied. There was short awkward moment where it went completely silent as they stared up at the sky. As she was still looking up he looked over at her and she could feel a pair of her eyes on her so she turned to look at him. Their eyes met and he spoke up "I am not your enemy I hope you know that, you don't have to be afraid of me." He said to her and she nodded in agreement.

"You have been afraid of me for so long and I know that then when you found out I that I am Roderick you freaked even more. I don't want things to be awkward, not in my own house. I am your friend, well to me you were my friend and you've always been. You are the one who did not want my friendship even though you could still have other friends alongside Rocket if he was not so controlling." It was a bit sensitive to hear about it coming from him but it was time for her to hear him out because she did not hear him even though he constantly hears her out and sees her, the real her. She finally decided to speak up "I messed up, I did not appreciate all the good things that I had received and ruined my dad's friendship with your dad and also you. I took that away it was all *my* fault." She emphasised. "It is not your all your fault, I didn't speak up I chose to run away and that was not right either." He looked at her and then was a silence for a moment before she chose to speak up.

"You deserved better not what we gave you, all the hell we gave you that was not fair at all. Look at you though, you got better. You won." After she said that he looked directly into her eyes and said "No, I did not win, everything." With that he got up and walked back towards the house.

Stella was left confused with that statement as she continued to open up her diary and write in it but rain was pouring and she had to get inside so she left her writing for another day.

When she went in she saw Francis sitting with Agnes at the couch and they greeted each other. Francis was busy on his phone so she went to her room to place her diary right before she went to clean up the gym and office. She could not wipe the words Francis said to her earlier as it kept playing in her mind. *What didn't he win?*

*What was it that made him feel like he had not accomplished much when clearly he has achieved so much?* It was really hard for her to understand what he means at times as he speaks with underlying meanings with no direct point that is understandable to her. She was cleaning the same spot for way too long because of her deep thoughts until she was snapped back into reality by Bella who noticed she was not really paying attention to what she was doing. She went over and placed her hand on Stella's shoulder to get her attention.

Stella was startled by her and almost fell down. "My dear girl what is on your mind? You are not here." Stella could not reply her at that point and stayed silent as she stood up. "I am not fine Bella. I've been thinking about my conversation with Francis he said he did not win, everything when I told him that he is doing quite well considering what he went through and I feel that I have done something wrong through his response but I do not know what." After hearing that Bella started giggling quite discreetly. "I'm glad you find my confusion hilarious M'lady." Stella replied to her. "Still darling, sweetie. I would say what I feel but I rather not certain things need to come from the horse's mouth for you to understand clearly. Sometimes when we look at people we need to *SEE* them not just look. When we see them we will understand what is really on their mind."

Bella replied her. Stella looked her in the eye and said "Now, I don't understand you." They both laughed after a short pause in a serious moment. "Really, need to understand him more the way he understands me." She was caught up in her thoughts as she spoke. "That is because he *sees* you more than you can *see* him." With that she walked away and left Stella in more confusion. It frustrated her to never understand the deeper idea of the points that people are trying to bring across to her.

She tried not to accept what she thought she understood and she wanted to leave it in her thoughts where they were. She was already absolutely confused by everyone's underlying meaning based conversations. It was exhausting enough to hear it from them. Stella, the over thinker did not need more thoughts to be filled with for sure. She had other things to worry about and this was not one of them. Her heart already been broken by one man and also the death of both her parents, she did not need for it to be broken further with unnecessary feelings. Anyway, most importantly the next day she had to go down to the campus where she was about to be a student at and it was nerve wrecking after not studying for years. Her overthinking drifted to that instead of the previous topic and she wondered if she would ever fit in. It took a lot of energy out of her spending her whole day thinking and thinking with more thinking.

Later that night, she prepared her bag with stationery and her documents that were required for the entrance test and more importantly admission if she were to do well in the test. She had to be up by 6am and Ren was already scheduled to drop her off at the campus.

Tucking herself into bed and hoping she could get some sleep became her daily routine. The poor girl struggled to hold herself together due to a lack of mental rest and it was not easy for her to focus especially at this point of time she really required that focus. The next morning or rather a few hours later she dragged herself out of bed, into the shower, to dress up and be ready for Ren to pick her up. She waited outside at the porch and Ren's car did not pull up at the front but it was Francis's car that pulled up. He looked at her and she looked at him after he rolled down his windows to signal her to get in.

It was awkward pause yet again but she broke the pause and entered instead. "I thought Ren was picking me up." She said to him. "I told him to take the day off his family needs him."

He replied as he focused on the road. He sped through the whole drive as his music was blasted so it would make things less awkward between them. They reached the destination really fast due his amazing speed without limits. Stella thanked Francis before exiting from the car and for the first time as shocking as it was he smiled at her. *His smile is beautiful* she thought as she smiled back at him. She turned and entered the campus to go register for the entrance test. As she sat at her desk after the registration process was complete in her heart she thanked daddy for the sacrifice that he had made for her and she prayed before she had begun her test. Her hard work came from being inspired by her daddy.

He had worked hard all his life to build a better life for everyone he called family even if they were not blood related. Her doing well was just so she contribute to being a result of his sacrifice and hard work. So that in the near future she could be a source of blessing to other people like daddy was. Every question seemed to be within her favour except the last one. She was perspiring as she sat in front of the paper with the question staring at her, struggling to answer it and under her breath she prayed that she may receive the grace to answer. She did what she could and once it was completed she was asked to wait outside while it was being graded. Waiting time is not very pleasant when you are not sure what to expect. If she were to fail the entrance test she would be given a second chance to do it but that would mean she would have to waste another precious day on that. Stella really hoped that she would get the grades that she needed now.

"Stella Marie." The receptionist called out to her and asked her to go in and see the teacher. "Please have a seat, I am Mr Simon and I am the one who graded your test, you sure you did not study for so long? You sure did really well for someone who has not." He said to her and a smile quickly formed on her face. "You're in welcome to Anderson college. We hope you achieve what you could not before and pursue a great career after your time with us."

Stella Marie's heart leaped with joy and she was so grateful for the fresh opportunity she was going to step into. After her completed meeting she decided to head back on her own but she saw Francis's car parked out front and he was waiting for her. "Hey, did you wait around all the way? I was gonna head back myself." She said to him. "I drove around a bit let's go." They both got into the car and Stella went on and on about her excitement to be admitted into Anderson college. This was the first time she talked this much to Francis as he listened fervently. "I have never done so well in a test before because I was so caught up with a lot of other things. Thank you for supporting this and me, I don't deserve it." She was grateful so she needed to put it into words and let him know how much it actually meant to her that he came along for the journey. As he stopped the car to drop her off as soon as they reached home, he turned over looked at her and said "I want you to prosper in life, Stella Marie and I am just doing what I can to help that happen. You're a good person which you've always been.

Start your journey to your own success and I mean basically start your journey of life. You paused it for so long it's time for you to explore it further. Find you and be you. You have no one left to sacrifice for at this point except *you*." Francis emphasised to her. "Now, get out of my car I am running late." He said and she quickly did so which left him laughing softly seeing her freak out. He then drove away as quickly as she got out of the car.

Bella and Agnes were waiting patiently for her and were absolutely thrilled with the fact that she got in! She was going to be student again and it was a new direction for her since all the years of just focusing on daddy and being a housekeeper. Daddy gave her so much to rejoice about and that is support her future even after he was gone. He took the time to care and help her reflect on the person she had to become in order to be more focused and to procrastinate less. A better version of herself indeed to go in and complete tasks without leaving them halfway done or just undone. Directions give you a path to follow, the path to follow gives you focus and focus gives you a final destination to immersed in.

She needed to be immersed in something in order to completely pick herself up from being broken and down because Stella Marie was not a quitter in her mind. She may not always have it altogether out in the world but she never gives up trying. She fights just like she fought for daddy and receive time with him right before he was taken away completely. As she sat down with the ladies to talk about her entrance test she saw the joy and excitement on both their faces as if they were the ones who went for the test. It is really hard to get people who are truly happy for you in a lifetime without any underlying selfish needs. "I did really well and I will be starting class next week as the new term starts." When she said that Bella and Agnes hugged her with so much excitement. "We believed in you from the start and are so happy you are finally getting a head start on doing something for yourself. You truly deserve it baby." Bella was thrilled to say. Stella had a small chat session before all of them went about their business for the day. She asked for permission from Francis to call Marilyn and Jamie to let them know about progressing forward. They were of course, over the top excited to hear that their friend is finally furthering to build her future.

Francis was busy at his computer but he was also busy thinking about other things mainly how it was going to be different once he completely let's Stella go to pursue her career and move back into her own house that Marilynn and Jamie have been taking care of for her. As much as she was seeking out direction he was seeking it as well. He had great help from Bella even though Stella was just the extra help. Bella was getting older and he may need to look for someone new so she could finally retire and have time for herself. As he had earlier thought about quitting the entertainment industry and working with his dad. Direction took a lot of thinking and planning and it was not too easy. Stan Ray gave him good advice always but following it would always be his choice and clearly he had no idea how to at times. To think someone who has built so much success still has a hard time figuring out where to go. How much more for the girl who only knew one way? His thoughts drifted back to Stella Marie. He did care a tremendous amount for her more than she could ever know. He was truly going to help her every step of the way as much as he could.

She came in just as he was in deep thoughts to clean his office and he quickly went back to typing on the keyboard. Stella did not pay any attention to him either way she was just busy doing her work. Francis could see that she was focused or rather more focused because he was there but nonetheless focused.

When she was walking towards his table she tripped over the leg of a stool and fell directly at his feet where she spilled some detergent from her mini bucket on the tip of his really expensive pants that is when she freaked out. "OH MY GOD! I am SO sorry! I should have looked out..I." When she looked up she just saw his hand reached out to her to pull her up. He did not say a word or look angry. "You are not mad?" She asked him. "You are going to wash these pants for me so it'll be fine." He replied. He was so cool about it and he really did not feel mad at her as much as he wanted to be. She was obviously shocked at his reaction she expected to get a tongue lash but that was not the case. He was being gracious and at that moment she felt extreme relief that he did not react in anger or frustration. Francis knew that if he were to react that way it would just make her more fearful and push her away. "Could you put your stuff down and uh help me with something here." He said as he pointed out to his computer. She did as he said and went over. "I am getting you a laptop for college you can look at the choices here and choose one. I am not gonna cut your money it will be from me. Just choose and I will order it." She was shocked but really thankful for that offer.

"Thank you so very much I am so, thank you. I don't deserve this any of this after all I did to mess things up. I.." She tried to continue but he cut her off "Need to choose a computer quick, I don't have all day you know I need to meet with my producers later. So please choose and stop talking about the past. We all have regrets but we need to move on and that is the greatest direction forward we could ever take.

My dad always tells me this until today whenever I talk about everything I have lost." When he said that, he intensely looked into her eyes. She could not take hers off his for about 2 minutes straight. "Ok, i'll take this." She pointed to a Macbook pro and just like that he ordered it. "Ok I am heading out to meet my producers please stop living in your past." He said before he headed out.

"Boss, please....change your pants it has detergent." He stared at her and then headed to his bedroom to get changed. Stella Marie giggled to herself as he left. As she went back to the 2 minute *moment* that they had. She wondered if it really was a moment. Where was this thought leading her, well she certainly did not want to find out.

# CHAPTER TWENTY TWO

———⟐⟐⟐———

## *My Prize*

*Not all prizes are won right away,*
*they sometimes take years*

*A week later…*

Her previous week had been pretty relaxed as she was pumping herself up to go to college. It had finally come, her first day of college and it felt rather satisfying to know that she well on her way to build a future for herself. Mostly given to her by daddy and a little help from some angels in her life. As she carried her brand new laptop gifted by Francis she was so grateful to have the opportunity to walk the halls of Anderson College. It was night classes so she did not have to worry about bumping into younger kids or feeling embarrassed. Her teacher Mr Henry made them really feel welcomed and she met older students like Larissa who happen to be a 40 year old mother of 3 grown children. Rena who was already a grandmother and others in the early 20s or mid 30s. There were only about 20 of them in the class and it felt pretty good to meet these people from all different backgrounds and different walks of life. They were given an icebreaker to start off the day where they introduced themselves.

"Hi My name is Geoff I am 35 and after years of supporting my family I've finally been able to pursue my studies which I have been looking forward to do since I dropped out of high school."

"Hi I'm Mae, I have not touched a book for 30 years and here I am pursuing my dreams to study and become a counsellor one day."

When it came to her turn she became a little nervous to speak in front of a crowd of people she really was not used to. "Hi my name is Stella Marie, I'm 25 and I am here because my daddy believed in me and gave me this opportunity to study after all the years that he sacrificed for me and I gave some time back to him when he was sick and I did not finish my studies. So I am here to make him proud by doing something for me.That's what he sacrificed for my future."

Everyone applauded for her as she said that including the teacher Mr Henry. The introductory class went on really well and everything was easy to take in for someone who had not studied for the longest time.

She made some friends too and it was quite an amazing experience for her to have. Even though she missed her opportunity at youth she felt that this was good enough for her to have. Not many people even make it to college and she did and it was a real blessing to be able to experience this. It was getting really late and Ren was waiting for her so she quickly packed up to rush over to his car. "Well, dear college student how was first official day?" Ren asked her "I am really blessed and even though I don't deserve it I truly have had the best opportunity. Thank you for waiting." Ren received her thanks with appreciation. "Well, our boss really cares for people and my dear girl he cares for you a lot. I could have had more days off but I decided not to take it because he needs to work or else he'll be here, he still wanted to. He's not gonna let you take the bus." Stella smiled and she really felt that when Ren said it. Once she reached home she really felt exhausted. Even though she worked the entire day before going to school it was the mental capacity to take in everything she learnt on her first day that really tired her out but she was satisfied as well as happy. *Fulfilment.* Something every human craves for in order to feel like a prize has been won.

Many times loss is what a person understands and its not always by physical death but when relationships grow apart, when you don't get the opportunities you work hard for or let slip out of your hands. Many times in life we do that to ourselves *we* let things, opportunities or people slip out of our hands and we don't take responsibility for it, we rather blame others. Stella Marie has taken responsibility for her shortcomings which she has sacrificed many years for and she is a person who always takes responsibility for her actions. There are times after losing so much she just wanted to win sometimes, something that belonged to her so she wouldn't have to keep slogging for having a better life. She put in a lot of effort to stray away from bad habits like chasing after a guy like Rocket and putting all things there were not important as a priority over the things she was meant to prioritise. Now this time she had to change that and go for what is important and that is her goals that she had set aside to achieve a longtime ago.

To her, education has always been important but choices have always affected her from moving forward. Now, nothing is going to stop her from moving forward anymore. At least she really did hope so and she had to work hard for it. The prize is always in front of her eyes it is whether she notices it and walks toward it which is a problem sometimes for people when we do not notice the value of the prize we tend to walk away from it instead of walking towards it. Now she needed to keep in mind how important it was to be strong and courageous which she was ready to do. As the days went by, her time and energy had been taken up so much in the day that she was too tired and when she reached her bed she slept off immediately. She finally had sleep and less thoughts. That really was progress for her to be uplifted by. She might have been healing from anxiety at this point and lack of her mind playing up on her. It felt like a positive change even though it was so tiring. It gave her a sense of relief and rest that she had not had in the longest time.

Francis had spent the entire day with Agnes who was having a rough day because her ex was threatening her with unnecessary threats and putting her down. Though Francis wanted to intervene he respected Agnes decision for him not to. She knew her cousin would freak out over the matter and she was afraid of what he would do to the guy if he had the chance to interfere. It was very encouraging to have him by her side and he was very happy to have her by his. The brother and sister bond these cousins had is absolutely spectacular. Agnes knew that if she wanted someone to talk to who never judged her it always had to be Francis.

Stella was up and ready for work earlier than usual ever since she had started college. She had to be done early with her hours for the day so she would have time sit down and complete any assignments. Even though it had been just a couple of months she really had a lot of assignments to complete on a daily basis. Agnes could see her struggling to rush her work through when she walked past the gym that Stella was cleaning. "You know I could help you if you'd like right?" Agnes offered. Stella just laughed and told her that she did not have to. Agnes loved having around and since she did not want to socialise much with her friends since her breakup with her ex as they shared a lot of mutual friends and if she met up with them she would feel really pressed down.

"Hey if you were to leave this place after you graduate and get on with your career, would you forget about us, little people?" She asked jokingly and Stella playfully hit her on the shoulder. "Of course not, I got into college because of you guys and Uncle Stan. I could not be more grateful and I would not even dare to forget you guys.I have angels and you can never forget angels. Francis, he surprises me with his heart its so pure and caring. What more could you ask for? A boss like that who would go all out for you? I don't think I would ever get another boss like that." She reflected as she spoke those words. Agnes smile reached from one end to another. She was absolutely taken away by that sentence. "You know my mum used to tell me something and that's what helped decide to leave my fiancé other than the abuse, she said if someone really loved you, they would go out of their way not just one time but every time to make sure you are taken care of. They don't know how to express it in words so they do things for you. Even if it's out of their convenience." Stella listened attentively to Agnes.

"Well, I better go get some work done and leave you to yours sweet Stella Marie." Agnes placed her hand on her shoulder before she left the gym. Stella pondered on the things she said after she had left. Love was a really strong word, she was pretty sure that Francis's efforts was just care and nothing more. Besides he was in the entertainment industry he could have anyone he wants. Why would he want her? It was ridiculous to even think about her boss that way, to her. It is definitely impossible. He was her childhood friend but times have changed and when people grow older how they thought as a kid changes as well. Stella rushed her work so that she could sit down and focus on her assignment that was due for the day. Studying really pulled her interest and gave her a good focus. It was helping her to heal from a lot of things. A source of diversion from all the things she is meant to let go of but has been holding on to for too long. Healing is a choice but sometimes people need a reason to push them so they allow themselves to heal. Studying and a future stable career was her reason but maybe it was not going to be her only reason. She had to move on from Rocket one way or another. He already did so it was time for her to let go of him completely from her system and find clarity in what she had accomplished so far.

She had a lot to be grateful for as of late and it had to be a constant reminder for her to find her absolution. Too much baggage had been storing up inside of her and this baggage could possibly block her from opening up her heart in the future. Or near future if the probability was there. No one wants to go their whole life holding on to baggage that had been left by someone else while they moved on leaving it behind. Stella Marie's life had been a series of unfortunate events so she became immune to the fact that something was always going to mess up the good part of her life. No matter how much she tried to stay positive there was always a thought at the back of her mind forcing her to think of the worst and sometimes she could not fight it. It was tea time and she caught up with Bella to prepare something for Francis's guests who were coming over to discuss work related matters with him. So they prepared something special. Though she had to rush over to complete her assignment and get ready to leave for school she still made time to help out in the kitchen. Bella was truly appreciative of the efforts that she had put in to always be there to help her when there was a lot to handle. They had a couple of part time kitchen staffs to help at times but Stella always helped out more so that they did not have to do much.

"I am going to miss my little *Elf* when she finally starts getting a career and flies away from us." Bella joked. "This little Elf just started studying so quite a long way to go. You're gonna be stuck with me for a longer time that you would like to think." Stella replied. Bella was so happy to hear that from her. "Well, for that reason, you better get a man I can get along with so I won't try to break you up because that will take you away from me too." She joked yet again. "I don't think I can really find anyone who would accept my history do you?" Bella put her utensils down and placed both her hands on both of Stella's shoulders and said to her, "You will find someone who sees you for you and not what you have, not what you have done or not what you do. So, don't think about your history, just appreciate you like all of us do." Stella felt encouraged by that and hugged her. They were almost done with the food when they heard the guests arrive. Both of them rushed out to serve them. Stella was done she quickly went to her room to get her assignment done then she got ready to go to school. Ren was ever ready to pick her up and drop her off.

She was thrilled by the friends she had already made who were all different ages and gave her a lot of things to talk about as well as ponder on outside of their study topics. Of course her best friend at this point had always been Bella but there was no harm in making new ones.

After class ended, everyone went their separate ways and Stella was expecting Ren to be waiting for her already so she rushed out but it was a different car and a different driver. "Hi, I..thought Ren would pick me up." Francis was at the driver's seat while Agnes was sitting at the passenger seat. "We are going for supper. Hop in!" Agnes said to her. "There is a burger place that is opened until twelve so we are going to head there." Francis stated. When they reached their destination Francis and Agnes asked her to wait in the car while they went to order takeaway as they decided to eat in the car because Francis was in particularly good mood or else they could forget it. As they ate and enjoyed their supper during an unholy hour well.. to eat, they had the windows down and it was really windy so he could save the power in the car. They spent almost 20 mins eating and chatting as all of them were fast to eat up their food. Agnes was particularly happily chatty and she said something that immediately created an awkward silence in the car. "Hey if you are single 10 years from now and you two never find anyone, would you date each other? Just curious." Both Stella and Francis had nothing to comment at that point. "Hey let's head back, I've got a meeting in the morning." Francis ended the awkward silence and buckled up his seatbelt and signalled them to do so too before he started the car. Agnes was a little taken aback by his reaction so she apologised for asking. Stella was just confused why the supper session that was supposed to be chilled ended so

Stella Marie, had not properly grieved for daddy or let go of the hurt that Rocket had caused but she held on to Bella's words to her earlier that day. Maybe that was a way for her to move on from feeling all the unworthiness that she felt to ever find love again. To move on with her life and build a better future instead of living in the past. How long can one really live in the past?

It only makes one a bitter person and never better. Bitterness can eat you up inside if you don't work on all the old wounds you have bottled up inside which Stella Marie clearly had to work on. She did not feel bitter but if she lets the hurt linger within her it will turn into bitterness. When they reached home Agnes apologised to both of them before heading up to her room. Stella Marie decided to sit at the porch and relax her mind. Francis was curious why she was sitting outside so late at night so he joined her. "Look, you can ignore what Agnes said it's not big deal, really." He kept silent and waited for her response after that.

"I am not affected by that I just worry that if I do meet someone else I will not be able to release the hurt Rocket left me with. I might hurt someone else and I do not want to that." She vented. "I think the other person just has to be mature about it and it'll be fine and you need to let go. Really, let go. It's easier said than done but I see you and I know you are trying." Was Francis's response. The word *I see you* is very strong and it holds so much meaning when someone says that. "He's not in your life, you need to let him go so you can finally see other things in front of you." His words made her to lift her head up and look at him. "Why are you so good to me? I was a terrible person to you. I messed up. I took the friendship we had for granted and ruined our dads friendship too. Im just glad they reconciled before daddy left." She said. "You can't ruin a strong friendship no matter what you do, their friendship was never ruined. I never stopped hoping you would change. Here you are." He added.

Tears rolled down her eyes when he said that and she could to control it. He wiped the tears off her face with his right hand and then he hugged her. After they pulled apart from the hug he continued speaking "Get out of it, kid you are strong enough. My mum always used to say, when I came home crying from all the bullying and then after the dance as well. I begged them to move me out of town but if all that did not happen I wouldn't be here right. Destiny led you right to my doorstep to fix things so allow it to be fixed." He made her realise. She looked at him with the biggest smile and gratefulness was written all over her face. This was the friendship she let go off for a Rocket but God was good to restore it back to her giving her this genuine person with a kind heart in her life.

"Let me win completely Stella Marie, I don't want to feel like I lack something. I don't want to lose you." He said to her and waited for her response. Stella was at a loss of words because she did not want to misinterpret what he was trying to say. "What do you mean?" She plainly asked him and he just looked away and smiled to himself. "You still don't get it? I like you but if you still can't get over your ex and don't like me back I am not going to force you. I do not want you to feel obliged if you have not completely moved on." With that he got up and went back into the house. Stella was taken by surprise because clearly she was oblivious to his long running feelings towards her.

This was definitely going to make things more awkward for her and she did not do well with awkward. Things were just getting comfortable with him and she did not want to mess it up any further. She did not know how to reciprocate his feelings when she has only been with one guy her entire young life and had no idea how to open up to another. She was afraid to trust another guy even though she knew his character, opening up was not an option at this point. It was only going to ruin a good friendship and good working environment. It was going to mess up everything she ever worked hard to build here even the focus on her studies. It would be affected if her heart got broken again by another guy just like it did when she was younger. Her thoughts suddenly started acting up and her panic attacks played up so she had to go in and get a glass of water. She found it hard to breathe so she took a sip of water and breathe deeply in and out. Bella heard someone in the kitchen and was curious to see who it was.When she turned on the light she turned on the lights she saw her Stella uncomfortably taking a sip of water and breathing in and out.

"Here, honey lets get you to sit up straight on the couch so you can take proper breaths in and out to calm you down. Come on!" She gently led her back to the living room towards the couch. As she rested Bella rubbed her back and got her to relax. Stella was trying to explain something but Bella calmed her down telling her not to speak and just to rest first. "Relax your mind, no speaking necessary, catch your breath first." Bella advised her as she continued rubbing her back and making her to drink warm water. After that she managed to calm down and breathe normally."Ok now, what happened child?

You were fine for the past couple of weeks." Bella asked her. Stella did not want to tell her at first but she was the one she confided in so she wanted to. "Francis, I mean boss and I were childhood friends right and things went completely wrong because I was too caught up with another person that I ended up being a bully. He moved away because he was young and the incident that happened really hurt him. Uncle Stan and my dad were best friends but their friendship was ruined on that day for years they did not talk. Long, story short Francis just told me he liked me and I did not say a word. He was respectful about my feelings so after that happened my overthinking caused this. I don't know how to move on from my first love because he was the only one I ever knew and he hurt me but it makes it hard to open up again." Stella confessed.

"Oh love, it's your life and if you keep yourself back in the past you are never going to be able to take whatever is waiting for you. I have known Francis since he was a kid and he has lived such a well disciplined life. He worked hard to become better in every way and when he cares for someone you know he goes all out. I'm not saying you have to choose him but I am asking you to open up your heart. Don't complete seal it or harden it because of your past." Bella advised her and then gave her a hug. Stella thanked her and after that she felt better so she went to try to get some sleep but she could not. She started crying and it everything felt so heavy like what Bella said, it was true her heart towards a romantic relationship had been sealed as well as hardened that she could not give anything a chance because of it. Her past still had a hold on her even though Rocket had already moved on it was not him who lost his child, it was not him who almost lost his father neither was it him who carried the guilt of almost killing her father because of a false statement at the courthouse. All that was in there and it never seemed to want to leave her.

When she cried all that suppressed emotions were let out, all that guilt, condemnation and failure hit her really hard. She fell to the ground as she had to control herself from screaming. It was painful and it literally hurt as she cried. In her mind thoughts of how she messed replayed like an old recorder. Everything swamped her mind at once and it was too much to take. She finally caved and screamed but controlled it by covering her mouth.

Bella heard her and quickly dashed into her room and held her without saying a word. She held her like she would hold a wounded bird in her arms. Bella teared too because she could feel her it was heavy and dark but she was not going to let her remain that way. Stella continued to battle her combined pain as she screamed her pain out but Bella never let her go. "I've been alone for a long time, I don't know what to do." Stella cried as she said that. *Unbearable pain.*It's not always physical the heavier your heart is once you break the pain you feel is completely unbearable until you are able to release it completely. *Broken, shattered and dysfunctional* is not supposed to be forever. It's supposed to be healed and let go of.

Bella lifted Stella up and got her to lie on her bed and tucked her in. She kissed her on her forehead before she left the room. Bella was wiping her tears outside of the door when she noticed Francis sitting at the couch. "You're up. It's late." Bella had another young heart to deal with and she was definitely not getting any sleep that night. Francis just looked at her and smiled as she sat by his side. "What's bothering you? I may know a little from a certain little bird because you know the little bird confides in me as well." She said and made him laugh a bit before his reaction went back to being serious. "She has been broken, young man. Her heart got ripped out of her and messed with. She had everything taken away from her so it's going to be a little harder for you." Bella made a sensible statement.

"When we were little, the greatest part of my weekend was meeting my friend. Going to her house, while our dads hung out and mums cooked together in the kitchen until her mum died. We talked, we played and it was fun. It was the highlight of my week because I did not really have any friends she was kind of the only one who really treated me like a friend but from Mondays to Fridays when we were at school, I was invisible to her. I was a joke to all of them even though I was the teacher's pet and they never let me forget that. Then, we would go about the same routine during the weekend again. Then it was the dance that messed me up if that happened to me today I would laugh it off or punch the lights out of everyone who did that but I was a kid.

Very vulnerable and it really hurt me that all that while I still considered her my friend but she was willing to do anything for Rocket even hurt someone who was nice to her." He vented and continued on.

"I won't lie and say it still doesn't hurt me because we crossed paths again so it definitely comes back, the memories but I can't help how I feel, I still care for her like how I did as a child it's really weird to me to that I am able to do that." Bella smiled at him and tapped him on the shoulder when he said that.

"That's who you are, you are a good person and you will always be. What is meant for you will eventually be yours if you hold on a little longer. Just give her time to heal and give yourself time too. It will all come together." Francis was very thankful for her uplifting words.

"Thank you for that but not too much time, Bella that would just mean I am being made use of. I can't wait forever for something that does not see me." He replied before he got up and went to his room. Bella understood his decision but now was the time she could actually get some sleep before another, comes down with a problem for her to handle. It was like handling the two kids of her own that she had. She loved Francis, Stella and Agnes equally. So basically she accepted 3 more kids into her life. It was satisfying to know that she was needed more than just a housekeeper as a mother figure. It brought satisfaction to her always to know that she was there for them just like she was present for her own even though she worked so hard. Both her kids were raised just as well and she never made them feel neglected ever. Bella only had hopes for the best of all the kids she cared about and she definitely made it very clear to them.

She went to get some rest but her mind was still worried about Stella and she hoped she would get past everything and rise up. The next morning, Stella woke up feeling really weak. Like all her energy had been sucked out of her because she spent hours releasing all the anguish she carried within her and there was a lot more where that came from with an additional worry of how she was going to face Francis after the conversation that they had the night before. She got ready to do her job and remembering that the first part of her job was to serve him breakfast daily was not going to be very easy now.

When she got to the kitchen, Bella greeted her and passed the breakfast over to her to give it to him but she noticed Stella was not comfortable so she decided to do it for her but Stella wanted to do it anyway because it was part of her duty after all. When she went to his office he was busy on face time with one of his dad's business clients so that made it easier for her to place it on his table and then silently leave. She did smile and let him know that she had placed his breakfast down for him. Before she left the office he did not respond to her but continued facing his computer. Stella felt a little sad that he did not respond to her but he was busy so maybe his mind was too caught about what he was discussing.

She went back down to find Agnes lying on the couch working on something on her laptop. She greeted her before she went on to do work. She was also swamped with assignments for the week and she feared not being able to complete them if she delayed her work any longer so she rushed and completed her daily duties before getting permission to get her assignments done. She locked herself in her room and focused on her assignments it helped her a lot. She loved doing research and learning about the human mind because she chose the path of counselling. It was really good to learn how to help someone else and it also taught her how to help herself. Dealing with anxiety and depression and a lot of other contributing factors to include what you had been hurt with since childhood and how bullying also affects a person's attitude as they grow. When she was reading that part she got reminded of little Roderick and how her actions along with her friends would have affected him. It did not occur to her how heavy something like bullying could affect the mind and heart of a person no matter how old they are. Being a child makes it heavier because not everyone is taught to treat another person in such a manner when they are young. Or rather it is not in everyone to be bully or pick on someone who has never hurt you.

People may keep quiet and not fight back but certain actions could cause a river of baggage that never gets healed if they don't work of it. Her future job was to help people who've been through different things in life and she had to start learning how to deal from her experiences. That way it's not just about theoretical understanding of things but a practical one. All this made her think a lot and remember a lot.

She was recollecting and realising from reading a lot that there are strong impressions that are left on people at times and it may never go away unless you give them a new perspective of you. Daddy always reminded her that she would be fine and that things that she went through are all just part of her journey that would shape her. Learning these things really opened up her mind to be more understanding of herself and of people around her. She needed to understand herself and others better. Being a counsellor you would need to connect with people on human level and it's not just listening and talking it would listening, understanding and advising. Right now, she realised that she would need to talk to Francis and not just pretend that their conversation and whatever happened never happened.

It was not right and she knew it. As she was focusing on her assignments and her thoughts time had caught up with her and she needed to get ready for school. Her days kept moving but she had to move forward as well not just in her academics or work related matters but also in her personal well being. Taking care of one's health also means mentally and emotionally. She was determined to accomplish that and she needed to start by opening up her heart and mind. How else do you release what needs to be released in order to win the prize that awaits you in life and it's not always a physical prize it could mean achieving personal well being to it's best. Stella Marie never had the chance to heal because she never gave herself one for so long. She suppressed everything and mistook it as healing. Everything was buried deep within her and when she broke she could really feel it trying itself out of her from six feet under. Spiritual death is everyday compared to physical death. She was spiritually dying and if she did not fix it, it will eat her up inside for good.

Condemnation, self-loathe, insecurity, unforgiveness, feeling unworthy are things that damage. Stella carried all these for years and years. She even carried condemnation for being born because her mother died so early and she felt if she wasn't born maybe her mother would live also a deep wound that was yet to fixed.

Her class lesson was yet another enriching moment for her to see where she had to opportunity to see from the outside how she needed to improve herself. Her teacher, Mr Henry asked them a simple question that got her thinking.

"Class, are you worthy of love? Do you believe you are worthy of love?" He asked and waited for a response from each of them. At that moment Stella was encouraged to speak up from within her. "I would like to say something from my own point of view, I do not think I am worthy of love. I lost what I loved and I am afraid that I would lose it again and it builds up wounds that make feel so unworthy. I don't know how to open up my heart anymore." The whole class listened to her intently and Mr Henry spoke up in response to her. "Stella, you are worthy of love and if you open your heart again you would be amazed and what comes in to your life and changes your perspective. You need to feel worthy before you tell someone else they are. The past should not determine your future but it should determine the strength it takes to rise up from the pain." Stella agreed to his point and he continued further to address the class.

"Each and everyone of us are worthy of love if you ever feel you are not you need to examine your heart and release the factor that is contributing to make you feel this way. You need to fix it." He completed. "So the assignment for today, I want all of you to write down in an essay format, why you should feel worthy of love. It will all be confidential only I will read it and give it back to you after it is graded. I would like to understand each and everyone of you that I am training.So this will be your home assignment take time and pour your heart out according to your own limit." Mr Henry had been a counsellor himself for a long time before he became a lecturer. Being in this class had given her a lot of confidence to speak up. She was excited about her assignment but she was also worried about writing it because it would take a lot out of her just to write her experiences down because she did not feel worthy at all.

Ren picked her up and dropped her off at home and she went straight to her room. She quickly went to get a shower before she started on her assignment.

As she sat down in front of the empty piece of paper to prepare to write she cleared her mind as well as her heart. It was gonna take careful thinking what she was going to pen down.

*I am worthy of love because I chose to change myself in spite of everything I had done. I did A lot of things in my life that I regret. The one I loved broke me and took everything away from me but I chased after him over and over again. He kept taking and taking but I never stopped giving in which made it my fault. If only I had seen the importance of everyone else and not only this one person I would have had a chance to see real love. I do not what that is yet but I know that sooner or later I will open my heart to be worthy of love even more. My past should not define my future and what I am worthy of now. I do not want to let go of something good because of the way I feel after something that was not good for me already left me.*

*I am worthy of love because people are willing to share their love and care with me. I need to appreciate it and cradle it for it is given to me non selfishly. Love is not selfish, it is supposed to be patient and kind. Why am I still holding back? I guess I never believed I could love any other after him. The only constant love was my father's but even he is gone but his love is shown to me everyday in many different ways. I never thought I was worthy of his either after a huge mistake I made but he told me otherwise. I need to open my heart and let love in again. Love that I don't deserve yet I am made to feel worthy of.*

*I am worthy of love because I chose to love others and it is beautiful to be loved back. To have an open heart and an open mind in the right way. Love sees you, the real you and never gives up on you even if you have closed the door on it a million times because you walked through the door, you thought was the right one. I am worthy to have second chance.*

With that she ended her essay and she read it back word for word. That would lead her to think about her worth. Being worthy was an action but knowing your worth was characteristic that she needed to hold on to.

# CHAPTER TWENTY THREE

———◦/◦/◦——

## *My worth*

*You need to understand your*
*worth and take charge of it*

s she sat down and had her breakfast, she realised what she
had written down made a huge impact on her thoughts.
The word *Worthy* is a strong word. To feel worthy she needed to
understand her worth. How important it was for her to find her
identity again. She had given up all these years to Rocket and to
her problems in life. She forgot that her life was always meant for
her to hold on to and to take charge of. Her emotions belonged
to her, he choices belonged to her, he heart belonged to her and
no one else. She was always to take charge of her worth and not
surrender it to anyone else. Unknowingly, she gave her worth up
to everyone else's needs but her own. This was her life, her destiny
and her love that she had to share. She just needed to take her
worth back, her confidence and her insecurities had to leave. If
she did not let it go it was going to lead her further down and even
take her life from her.

Stella contemplated suicide a lot even to the point of trying to
drown herself and poisoning herself which she really needed to
move past. She was not going to carry all her emotional baggage
into another person's life. She respected Francis enough not to
respond to his feelings when she knew she was not ready yet to
commit to another person. Though she should not take too long
because it would lead her to lose her chance with someone who
cared deeply for her. She needed to work on her self-esteem more
before she could do so. "Miss deep thoughts, when can I have my
coffee please?" She was interrupted by Francis who was standing

behind her she quickly jumped out of her seat and rushed to make him coffee. She was about to go up to his office but he was sitting at the couch busy with his phone so she serve him his coffee there. "Can we talk?" She asked him and he agreed straight away. "What's up?" He said as he looked up at her. His look was very intimidating indeed.

"Um..since no one is here yet. I am a mess inside and I haven't left my baggage behind its heavy and I don't want to put it on you because I think you deserve better and I need to work on myself but I know you can't be waiting forever. I messed up once with you, I don't want to do that again. I know I am worthy of love but I need work." She ended there and waited for his response and he just looked at her without saying a word. After a minute pause, he finally spoke up. "I know what I deserve and I know what is good for me. Life is about working through things and letting them go but I understand where you are coming from. I like you but we don't have to get into a relationship now I just want you to leave your door open and stop closing me out as your friend. That's all!" She nodded her head in agreement and smiled at him. After that and made his way up to the office he always gave her something to think about when he spoke to her.

Friendship is the most important beginning to any relationship it helps you to get to know a person better before you choose to be more than just friends. She had that with Rocket but they were kids and he was a kid who never grew up when it came to their relationship. There was a lot of naiveness involved and bad choices. She was not a teenager anymore neither was Francis who is definitely not *Rocket*. She needed to differentiate that. Bella came from the market and was chirpier then ever when she saw Stella. "How is my little princess?" She acknowledged her and gave her the biggest smile. "She is gonna be fine, my dear fairy godmother." Stella joked back with her. Bella was happy to see her with a positive energy in the morning after the previous night. She had so much tell her about school and the excitement she had talking about her assignments as well as her interactions with her classmates really brightened her up. "Well, you deserve happiness. To see you happy talking about things that make you laugh and smile makes me feel good." She was encouraged by Bella's words.

They had the the most productive moments when they had a good chat every time they worked together. Stella was majorly and constantly encouraged by Bella's positive vibes that was absolutely what she needed. Positivity was helping her to grow and move forward which is what she constantly needed.

There was a lot of unrest in her that needed to be calmed. She seemed to have a lot of distractions to help her ignore the unrest but not fix it completely.

When all that is going on it was hard to find a proper balance of feeling better about herself. She needed to fight herself to prove her worth also to herself. Her battles constantly was within her. All her suppression would one day turn to rage if she did not fix them at this earlier stage. She did not want to grow old looking like the worst person to be around with nobody and living alone.

No, she did not want to be alone for the rest of her life so she had to fix herself at this point. She had to release all the unsettled emotions and battles within her. She knew that very well but she was not doing a great job to move on. As she went for more classes in the in the month she became more learned and not academically but each class gave her and everyone else a life lesson which made her see improvement in her confidence. They had many role play sessions in class which helped her to open up and speak up. She spent years in silence because of Rocket she always let him speak first in every situation. She never fought back and always naive enough to listen to everything he said.

Now it was her time to shine, to speak up and to believe in herself. She could have a thousand people believe in her but if she did not believe in herself then there was no point. She worked hard on her studies as well as herself. Weeks went by and she was really seeing progress in herself. She received great grades in essays and assessments that she worked on. It boosted her self confidence up and shifted her focus but this time it was not just a distraction it was her acknowledging and working on her weak points. Agnes was ever present and helpful as well. She helped her through assignments and had great conversations with her. Which made her extremely grateful for her presence. Bella was busy back and forth as she had to attend to her son's wedding that was happening over the current weekend. Francis gave her time off and she could take a whole week off but Bella was loyal and she worked through whatever she could.

So seeing as how Bella was busy Stella Marie leaned on her own strength and a little help from Agnes every step of the way while Stan Ray was in the house for the week to spend time with his son. So Francis and him were out most of the time there was not much to avoid at this point.They had not had a real long conversation since the mini one they had at the living room a couple of weeks back. Time had moved so fast since then and Stella Marie had to move with it. She made a lot of progress and her attacks were lesser and mind was not so clogged with unnecessary thoughts.

They both were each other's go to girls and it was nice to to have that bond. Agnes always wanted a good friend to lean on but it had been hard for her to find a good female friend and she was grateful for Stella. "You know lately, Francis has been convincing me to open up my heart and try dating apps so I decided to give it a shot and I am talking to this guy right now and he's pretty cool. He is a doctor and he has 4 sisters so he knows how to treat a lady, well I hope. Would you try dating apps?" Agnes asked Stella who was not keen on Agnes doing that either. "Don't you think you need more time to build yourself up and not be so quick to move on?" Stella gave her an opinion. "What is wrong with moving on we all need someone we could lean on and not have to go through this life alone just because someone broke us." Agnes added.

That made Stella think really hard before she spoke any further. Even Agnes was willing to move on even though it was really too soon after her breakup. Definitely more open minded that her dear new friend but it had to be a personal choice not a forced one to open up a heart and let someone else in. "I guess it is true that you should not be alone for the rest of your life, but what if that someone that you choose to remind of you of your mistakes and regrets when you were younger." Stella said as she was in deep thought. Agnes noticed that she was a little distracted by her thoughts as she spoke. "Are we talking about someone we both, like let's say my cousin." She smiled as she said. Stella was shocked and jumped up from her seat. "What are you talking about?" She asked in surprise.

"Excuse me, don't you think, I notice things?

I know my cousin when he is into something or someone, he holds on to it for a long time and he never stops caring for it until there is an opportunity for him." Agnes confidently responded. Stella just smiled and looked away. Agnes moved closer and placed her hand on her shoulder as she spoke to her. "Don't wait for too long or you might lose what is meant for you." She said before she made her way to her room. All the signs kept pointing in one direction well, all the words kept pointing in one direction. Bella's and Agnes also if Marilyn and Jamie were informed about this they would jump on board of this ship. Stella was not thrilled that everyone was so supportive of Francis's feelings but she did not want to close the door fully. She had to move on for herself and not hold on to the pain that she had felt for so long.

The pain that Rocket left her with because it left a big void in her heart that is affecting her every decision to find love again. He seemed to be waiting for her but at the rate she was going she was about close the door. Stella asked for permission to go and visit her father's grave as she needed some time away to think. Ren picked her up and dropped her off there.

When she reached there she sat at his grave side ant and she cried all the pain that she buried deep within she let it all out. "Daddy, you always told me about my worth in you. How important I was and always will be to you. I just did not know how important I was to me. I put Rocket first that I forgot that I should mean a lot to me. My worth is as important to me as someone else was to me. I deserve to be loved not based on what I have done and what I have lost but because I chose to start afresh. I chose to forgive and to be forgiven so daddy, I am going to forgive myself for what I did to you.

For what I did to Roderick, for what I did to my baby. It was not my fault that mama died. I forgive myself for choosing Rocket over me and you. I forgive me, daddy. Please let me know you hear this I am forgiving me, in front of you and I am claiming my worth in front of you."

She continued crying as she spoke feeling the release she had not felt at all since everything fell apart. "Francis or Roderick as we called him back then, he cares for me. He has done so much for me and I have failed to be able to see past my mistakes to accept him. Daddy I ask for your blessings that I may move on. I love me daddy just like you always wanted me to and I…miss you a lot. This place is fresh. My loss is fresh but if I never move on I'll never make you proud daddy.

"She ended by placing a flying kiss from her and on his photo placed on the grave stone. Ren was there, waiting patiently for her. Once she was done he picked her up and brought her for a drive so she could wipe away all her tears and be refreshed. It was time to listen closely to her heart and find out what it needed for once. Daddy was not around anymore but he was definitely in the business of making her feel better whether he was or not. He was always watching over and listening to her as she believed that he would never let her down no matter what the situation was. It was a start of a self restoration journey that she really needed for herself.

# CHAPTER TWENTY FOUR

*Falling into place*

*Everything was finally finding its way around*

*Six months later...*

Time was moving really fast and she was so busy with school and work that she had no time to go through the motions anymore. Her mind was getting into stable conditions and she had time to examine her heart which made her feel really good about herself. She had not much worries left to hold on to because she was finding ways to distract herself and at the same time release. She had already slowly taken steps to forgive herself and be more confident of what she needed and wanted. There was a difference in that and she took charge of her emotions and the condition of her heart. The condition of heart included the choice to open it up again to someone who cared for her needs more than his own. There was no comparison between Francis and Rocket.

They were absolutely different characters and had opposite characteristics which included being selfish or selfless. From the whole journey here she saw so much selflessness in Francis that she could not even comprehend. The past six months she was going through a self help journey that really gave her the confidence to rise up from everything she had been through. She was not going to hold back anymore and maybe come clean to Francis about her feelings. Her heart has been feeling things that she had not want to recognise but she did anyways.

As she fell into a deep sleep after a full on tiring day she had a dream. In that dream she saw daddy and her mama. They looked young and they were sitting and talking to each other when she had walked down the stairs they both looked and smiled at her. Though she did not have much of a memory of mama she looked as if she did before she passed. "Sweetie, I want you to have all that you never imagined having."

Her mama said to her and her daddy added on, "Baby Piglet, listen to your heart and open up at your mind at times. You will not be able to live your best life, if you make your path so narrow. We Love you Stella Marie." He said and her mama added, "We will always love you but you will have to love you more." With that her alarm rang and she woke up from a really good night's rest. She had forgiven herself but maybe she really did not love herself enough and she had to do that for her. Francis was waiting for his morning breakfast and she had prepared more than she usually did for him as she was finally going to speak to him about how she felt. Provided he had still been waiting for her with an open heart for six months since they had the talk. He had not been communicating very well with her for the past six months since both of them had been really busy. The only time was when Agnes needed to both of them on her date which made her meet someone she actually liked and had been seriously dating for five months. They clicked on the spot and he has really made her very happy ever since, no it was not a rebound it was a good kind of restoration that made her overcome everything that she had been through.

Meanwhile, Stella thought she would just go for it and talk to Francis. As she served him his breakfast she asked if he could spare sometime to speak with her and he agreed to. "I..um I have another six months in this course and I get to do some other job before I further my studies after that. I don't have to be your staff." Francis cut her off before she could continue. "What is your point? Can you get to it?" He said in frustration. "I gave myself time to heal and to let go. I gave myself time to be ready to let you know that I like you too. If you still have a place for me in your heart." She continued. He looked at her with no reaction at all. She was afraid that it was too late for her to let him know how she felt from the way he reacted.

"You would have to pay rent." He said and it confused her. "I may not be staying here so I do not think I need to pay rent." She replied and that made him laugh which caused her to be more confused. "I meant a place in my heart would cost you rent because you took up too much time and space there. It was not fair to both of us." He said and the biggest smile filled his face as he looked back down. She smiled too until he got up and walked towards her because that made her nervous.

As he moved closer to her she started to shake and he held her hand and stopped it from shaking. "The day you asked me to the dance was more special than the actual day. That I was willing to forget that day just to be able to make you my servant and pay for it but then I realised how painful life had already been and I was not going to make it worst but much better instead. No matter what you did, none of those actions were by choice but you were blinded and no you were let off scot free but you faced the pain you did. I did not have to add to that." As they looked into each other's eyes she cried because she was thankful that he had not shut the door on them. "Hey Rod, you really were my best friend and you still are. You did things for me that no one else would in your place. You're quite amazing though no one will ever live up to daddy, for me. You're halfway there." She joked. Francis leaned in and held her face as he kissed her softly and pulled apart. "You deserve to be treated like a queen Stella Marie. You are a gem and you deserved to be loved, you gave so much of yourself away to the wrong places that did not deserve you. You did great by taking of your father and nursing him back to health and journeying with him through his cancer. Though Rocket did not deserve you, he was lucky. If I ever mistreat you, tell me or walk away from me. Love should not abuse you but treat you with respect." Francis encouraged her with words that reminded her of her strength. He carried a beautiful character that reminded her of daddy's.

Daddy was always apart of her heart as she journeyed further through life with a second chance at a romantic relationship that uplifted her and made her stronger not dependant. Francis always reminded her of her identity the way that daddy did and *no* they were not to be compared but the quality that they carried was what she needed constantly in her life. She had learnt to let go and move on and in return she fell more in love with herself as well as the man who waited for her patiently. Months had passed, Stella had she finally completed her course and was ready to leave her job as a house keeper and finally go back to her neighbourhood, her own home though she was in a relationship with her soon to be ex boss. She had a house full of people rooting for them from the start so it did not feel like a struggle at all and it all came to an amazing change.

"Hey Stella, I kind of need you to go to the office to pick something up for me from Francis.I am kinda lazy to go up there. " Stan Ray who had been in town for the week was working hard and Stella knew that he was really tired and she most willingly offered to help him. "Sure, Uncle Stan I will get it for you." When she went up to the room Francis was out in his balcony that had an absolutely beautiful view especially since it was late in the evening.

"Hey, your dad needed me to.. Agnes, Bella is everything okay? Where is Francis." She realised when he was not sitting in his office. "Why is he out there? Is he mad at me for something?" She feared as she she asked. Bella just gestured for her to go over and speak to him which she immediately did. He was facing the view from his balcony when she went out into the balcony to greet him. He standing there staring into a really great view.

"Rod, are you okay? I told I would come visit even after I leave." She reassured him after assuming that her leaving was why he was quiet." Stella Marie," He turned to face her as he called out her name. "Let me cut to the chase with a little long winded speech." Stella was confused by what he was saying and so was he. He was trying to figure what to say at this point so he got down on his knee which made Stella really surprised. "I have no more words to say and I did not prepare myself for this but I cannot let you go. Will you be mine forever?Will you marry me?" He asked as he pulled out a ring from his pocket. Stella was speechless and then she got down on her knees and hugged him as she said yes. "I'll be glad to marry my best friend, that's you by the way." She said as she hugged him and cried. Agnes and Bella stood by in joy as Stand Ray walked in. He went over, pulled both of them up and hugged them. "Nathan would be smiling down in joy." He said. Bella and Agnes ran over and hugged them too. Stella excitedly called her friends Marilyn and Jaime when she had some time to. They were ecstatic when they heard that their friend was finally getting her very own fairytale after what she had to go through including all the sacrifices she endured.

*A year later on the 19th of July*

It was 1 year and eight days ago that she had lost daddy but it was also a special day for her. It was the day she was getting married to the love of her life. The made who made her better woman as did she make him a better man. They dated for a over year but they cared for each other way longer than that. She was in a white dress with her bridesmaid helping her out as her makeup artist worked on her. Yup, that was Bella. They chose to have a small little ceremony out in the backyard of Francis's home. It was beautifully decorated and it felt simple yet classy. Stella was just happy with the man she was going to spend the rest of her life with after spending a few years working for him.

It was going to be a whole new road. She was finally marrying someone who loved her as much as she loved him. Who gave her choices and made her feel like a woman every single day. It had been a year and he never changed the way he treated her. He also gave her choice to walk away if she were to be mistreated by him. "So, my precious little Stell Sweetie, you are getting married!" Bella gushed as she did her makeup for her. "You are marrying a wonderful man, Stella. He has a heart of gold and he has not changed that since I have known him. Which is a long time." She reassured her.

"Your daddy will be so proud of you for moving on and giving love a chance." Stella started crying as Bella stayed that. "Oh, honey I'm sorry, how insensitive of me? I should not have.." Stella cut her off and told her it was okay. "I am okay, I'm just missing him. He's not going to walk me down the aisle and it would have been the best thing to have him here, physically." Bella comforted her as she teared. She then touched up her makeup. Agnes came in to inform them time had been catching up. Stan Ray was waiting at the entrance to walk his future daughter in law down the aisle taking the place of his best friend. He was going to give her away to the bright young man that he raised.

As soon Stella was ready she held on to his arm and they walked in to the sound of *the wedding march.*

All her loved ones were sitting on her left as she walked in with grace and stature. She felt like a princess with the closest father figure she had right now walking her down th*e aisle.* Her dashing groom was waiting at the altar for her. As she was released to stand by his side her heart skipped a beat literally as she felt so much comfort knowing she had finally made a good decision in her life. As the priest spoke and they exchanged vows Francis could not take his eyes off of her and it neither could she take hers off of him. She wrote a special vow for him and prepared a special time to read it to him.

> *To my husband to be,*
>
> *I am blessed and I am very touched by the blessing of you in my life. You made me feel special every single day. I could not be more grateful for your life. You are an amazing human and I could not ask for better, My love, Francis.*
>
> *Your,*
> *Stella Marie*

After she read the vows they finished up the whole thing with *You may kiss the bride* very excitedly. The reception was a gathering of one big family. A bunch of people they both loved from each side of the family.They would spend the next few months enjoying each other's company and building their futures together. Francis had quit the entertainment business after a couple of months from their wedding. He full on focused on his dad's business which he enjoyed building. Stella Marie supported him as he supported her newfound career as a counsellor. She was under training but caught up really fast and she was absolutely good at it. There was never a day she forgot daddy in everything she did. He was the highlight of her life choices and he made everyone of it better. Daddy's memory always lived within in everything she did even becoming a mother which was her next step. After a month into the marriage she found out she was pregnant and four months after that she found it was a boy. She and Francis both agreed that his name would be Nathan Ray. With an essence of both their father's names.She carried her first son in her stomach as she went to visit her parents grave sides and placed a flower in Nathan Ray's name.

Stan Ray was obviously going to spoil his grandson on both their accounts that was his promise to Nathan as of late. He bought so many things for his grandson even before his birth. There was literally no space in the child's room left. He was more excited than the parents themselves that he spoiled him even before he made his debut into the world. "Dad, don't you think this is a little too much stuff, it might end up in goodwill." Francis joked. Stan Ray gave him a look that made him regret that joke he thought was funny.

"My grandson needs the world like I gave my son and even more so because he is also my best friend's grandson and I'm doing this for both of us." He pointed out and Francis hugged his father and thanked him. When he turned around he saw his wife fidgeting in the kitchen doing something and he excused himself from his father to go check in on her. "Now, what do you think you are doing? Bella said to call her if you needed anything." He said to her in a frustrated manner as he did not want his pregnant wife to be over exerting herself.

"Look, I am pregnant, not disabled." She responded and rolled her eyes before she went back to her room with an egg sandwich that she made for herself. Francis remembered how utterly stubborn she was and just let it go. Bella went into her room and stayed by her side massaging her leg and chatting with her when she had some down time. "Francis is upset that you did not ask for my help, to make a sandwich." She laughed as she said.

"I know he is looking out for me but I have always done things for myself and…" Bella cut her off before she could finish. "It is time for you to stop being so overly independent." Stella smiled at that comment and allowed Bella to clear her plate. Over the course of months she had great support from the family that she now has called her own. Agnes was in and out of the house that whenever she was around she pampered Stella Marie to the core. Stella was very grateful for her presence and help always. It made the day of labour feel so much more relaxed and not so alone.Time was moving really fast and May 20th finally arrived. Nathan Ray Lee, finally made his debut and he was just like his father. As she held him in her arms she was grateful that she was able to give life to another and this time he was born into a home filled with love, where he was going to be protected and taught well.

He will be raised to respect women and not use them. He will be raised to love and not hate with no discrimination of any. He will never be a bully but someone who stood up for the right things. This is what she and Francis instilled in their minds to raise a man and not a monster. A monster ruined her life and his at some point so they were going to raise a man who had a heart that could not be easily messed with and that heart will take care of another heart and treat her like a queen, not like a slave. That he was not to do anything against her permission but to respect her decision. That he was not to ever take advantage of her or manipulate her in any way. That love was not only about intimacy but it was more than that. It is about understanding and facing the giants together. To put others needs before your own at times but to also know that you deserve to love yourself in the process not at the expense of another but through your own abilities to show you that self love.

It was not just about instilling that into a girl but also into a boy. Like they believed not to raise a monster but to raise a man who had compassion as well as qualities that would make the world a better place for a girl to feel safe. This is what going through pain does, it is supposed to teach a person to build a better tomorrow and not to repeat the same mistakes. Life was about learning through being teachable from the right sources.

Stella Marie had been through so much that she did not want her next generation to face the world as she did. Being a mother was another journey of selflessness. It meant doing things beyond you to make life safer for another being. She was proud of the moment she could do that for her little one.

*Three years Later*

A three year old Nathan Ray Lee along with his parents welcomed his baby sister Mary Renee Lee. Life had given her more than she could ever imagine. It restored everything she had lost but better.

She had nothing to regret and nothing to feel guilty about anymore. She had the release she needed with family of four. They moved into a smaller home just nice for the four of them near to Stan Ray and Bella went home to her family after finally retiring but visited them every once in a while. Agnes got married and had a kid of her own whom she would always bring over for playdates with Nathan Ray and Mary Renee. Marilyn and Jaime also had kids of their own. Stella had a family to call her own that she never ever had to feel alone again and she was finally far away from the memory of her past as she learned how to smile everyday, appreciating life as it was. Daddy's strength always carried her through on her weak days. Remembering how he raised her on his own while she had so many people who loved her surrounding her. She was truly blessed to overcome all her dysfunctions a she did. Her gratefulness stayed strongly rooted in everything daddy had taught her in this lifetime.

Daddy was, is and always will be her rock in every way even after he was gone his words and wisdom remains to be her strength. She and Francis have their bad days but she has the best friend she could ever ask for in him. Life will never be perfect but when we learn to appreciate, to be teachable, to forgive ourselves and others we tend to learn how to live our best life.

We need to accept that we can never be perfect that we would aways mess up in one way or another but we need to rise up from it. First things first, Love yourself and forgive yourself for things you cannot go back and change but do better after that. Stella Marie if she never forgave herself or opened up her heart the way she did. If she never fought for a better life she would have spiralled down the path of death that would have never given a peace of mind. She would have been more negative if she had not had the positive influence around her like Bella or Agnes. As well as her good friends Marilyn and Jaime. Everyone made a positive impact on her whereas Rocket and his father were a lesson to her. A lesson well-learned. Never to hold on to what needs to be let go off. There is no need to cry over spilt milk but rather wipe it up and keep moving until you get a brand new box of it. One where there is strength and growth in every path. Stella Marie did so what are we waiting for? It starts with healing from what broke you.

**The End**

# BIBLIOGRAPHY

AUTHOR: ASHLEY V
TITLE: RETRACE
PUBLISHER: PARTRIDGE PUBLISHING
2020
SINGAPORE
*YEAR 2020*
*179 Pages*

# ACKNOWLEDGEMENTS

*First of all I would like to thank God for guiding me through this less than perfect journey. It took me a long while to be able to pour my heart into this. A lot of distractions and basically life, delayed this process. I would like to thank a dear friend who supported me in this process in more ways than one. She knows who she is and she played a big part in allowing this book to come together. To all those who encouraged and supported an amateur writer in her journey. This story is based off a person who was dear to me. It started out as her story but her real life ending was less than perfect but I would like to dedicate this book to Stell darling who was a real person who went through real situations that made her stop believing in love.*

*She could not forgive herself or move on from her past but she was a beautiful person who was never given the chance to be understood correctly. Her life ended abruptly but her love lives on. She was selfless in every way and she never stop fighting for those she loved until her last breath. A person who was clearly under appreciated until she was gone.*

*She suffered violent abuse but she never left the side of her kids no matter what. She put them first even in her pain. This is just a shadow of what could have been. It's a lesson for a woman or man to appreciate themselves and see their worth above all the blindings of love. It is not love when there is abuse involved and it is not love if you need to be manipulated. Be strong and Courageous in everything you choose to do and know what your worth is.*

Printed in Great Britain
by Amazon

31948625R00118